A Matter *of* Mind

An Introduction to the Art of Wladyslaw Dutkiewicz (1918-1999)

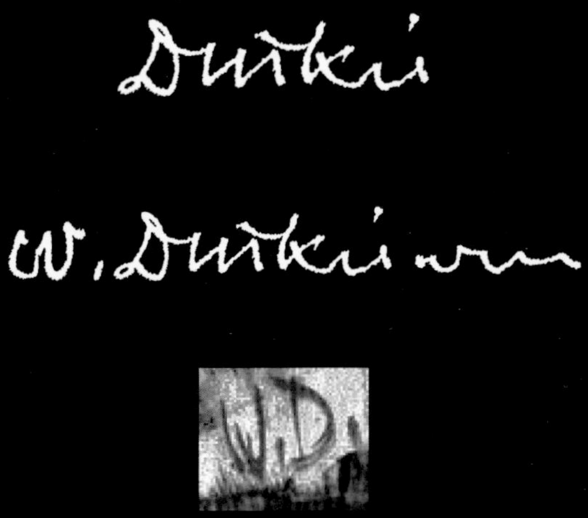

Adam Dutkiewicz

with Preface by
John Jefferson Bray
Interview with the Artist
Explication by Brian Claridge
and Biographical Chronology

Moon Arrow

Moonarrow Press
Box 3072 Norwood
South Australia
Australia 5067.

First published in 2006, edition 1000 copies.

The Dutkiewicz Archive is located in the State Library of South Australia.
Details are catalogued online in the Archival Database, Search Number PRG1385.
Photographers' credits are given when known.
Photographic prints for scanning: Duckpond.
Printed and bound by Tony Kitchener Printing,
40a Nelson Street, Stepney, South Australia 5069.

National Library of Australia Cataloguing-in-publication data:

Dutkiewicz, Adam, 1956 - .
A matter of mind : an introduction to the art of Wladyslaw Dutkiewicz (1918-1999)

Bibliography.
ISBN 0 9775455 0 4.

1. Artists - Australia - Biography.

709.2

Dedicated to the late Peter Mathers, a Worthy and Angel of Words.

Thanks to :
Alex and Pat Cmielewski for initial funding assistance and encouragement; Barry Dangerfield for financial assistance and unbridled enthusiasm; Graeme Hastwell for untiring efforts in photographing work; Jim Trice and Brian Danilko for computer assistance and maintenance; Dr. Thomas Loveday, Donna Brett and Tony Catalano for helping develop ideas; Stuart Collins and Roger David for their documentary films, the former also for some photography; Dr. Stephanie Schrapel for exhibition text development, curation and photography; Josef Cieslinski, Lydia Groblicka, Ivan Rehorek and Herbert Neetzel for research and assistance with translations; Cecylia Veldre for providing information and hospitality, and to Danny Whidden for his summary of her plight during the war; Andrew Steiner, Barbara West and the late Terence Stapleton for theatrical recollections; Penelope Hetherington for helping my father as model and collector, and for her correspondences and participation in documentary film; my doctoral thesis supervisors Dr. Catherine Speck and Prof. Ian North; Dr. Christine Nicholls; Dr. Bogumila Zongollowicz for documentary photography, filming and editorial and translation assistance; Barbara Fargher for editorial and layout suggestions; Charles Nodrum for advice and editorial and layout suggestions; and finally my family, including my wonderful mother, Joan, recently departed, and Ludwik, Michal, Anna, Ursula and Cecilia Dutkiewicz for their feedback, generosity and support.
A special thanks to all the people in cultural institutions, especially June Edwards, Diane Honey and Neil Thomas at the State Library of South Australia; Dianna Dahlitz, Acting Curator, Oral History & Folklore, National Library of Australia; Sarah Thomas, former Curator of Australian Painting & Sculpture, Art Gallery of South Australia; Gail Greenwood, Director, Flinders University Art Museum and her predecessor, Doreen Mellor; Erica Green, Director, University of South Australia Art Museum; numerous office holders of the Royal South Australian Society of Arts Inc., especially James Raggatt and Bev Bills; commercial galleries and auction houses who have been supportive, and to all the artist's collectors and admirers who have contacted me and often allowed me to see works in their homes.

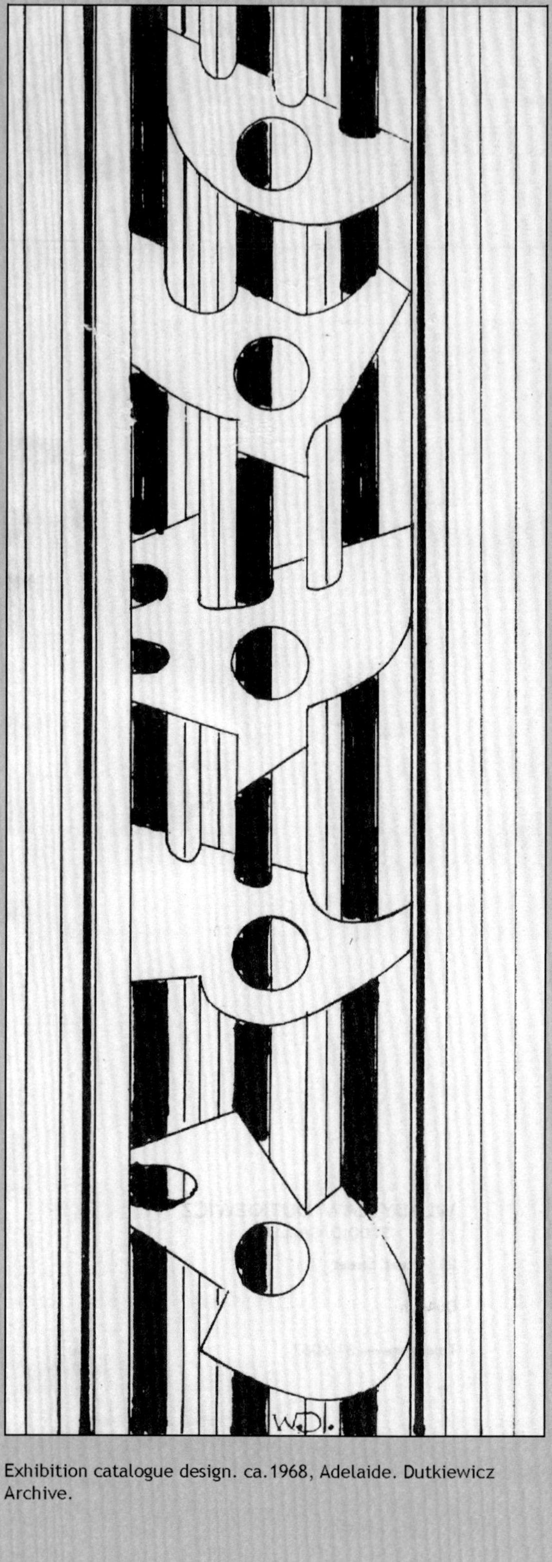

Exhibition catalogue design. ca.1968, Adelaide. Dutkiewicz Archive.

"Wladyslaw Dutkiewicz has produced work for which the appropriate standard of reference and comparison is the major group of artists ... Danila Vassilieff, Sidney Nolan, Dobell, Drysdale, Arthur Boyd ... There seems little risk in saying that this painter is more accomplished and exciting than either Dobell or Drysdale ... The whole of contemporary art is grist to his mill ... he is alive to all its facets, just as another of his virtues lies in the constant vitality and vibration of his visual sensibility."

Max Harris,
writer, 1951

"No visitor should leave Adelaide without seeing the depth and scope of the work of this leader of the contemporary movement."

Paul Beadle,
artist, art critic, 1960

"Dutkiewicz lets emotion rip; though he is far too professional a craftsman ever to indulge in the mindless orgies of the extreme abstract-expressionists."

Geoff Dutton,
writer, art critic, 1961

"There is ... a vigorous plasticity in Dutkiewicz's large oils, a rich orchestration of colour, expressing usually ideas ... sometimes discernibly figurative – tolerant, observant comment on human nature."

Elizabeth Young,
art critic, 1968

"Dutkiewicz's supreme importance as an original artist in his own right and as part of the texture of South Australian art is at last being recognized."

Ivor Francis,
artist, art critic, 1974

"Dutkiewicz's contribution of powerful abstract impressionist pieces ... should never be forgotten."

Ian North,
art critic, curator, ca.1975

"The best influence of the lot was actually Wladyslaw Dutkiewicz."

Ruth Tuck,
artist, art critic, 1985

"... a person of great stature both as an artist and as a man,
and we have reason to be proud that he became a member of this community."

The Hon. Dame Roma Mitchell, AC, OBE
Governor of South Australia
Letter to author upon the artist's death, October 1999

„Sztuka była dla niego najważniejsza ... Malarstwo było jego pierwszą miłością. Drugą – teatr."

("Art was most important for him ... Painting was his first love. Then came theatre.")

Dr. Bogumila Zongollowicz,
writer, journalist, November 1999

Contents

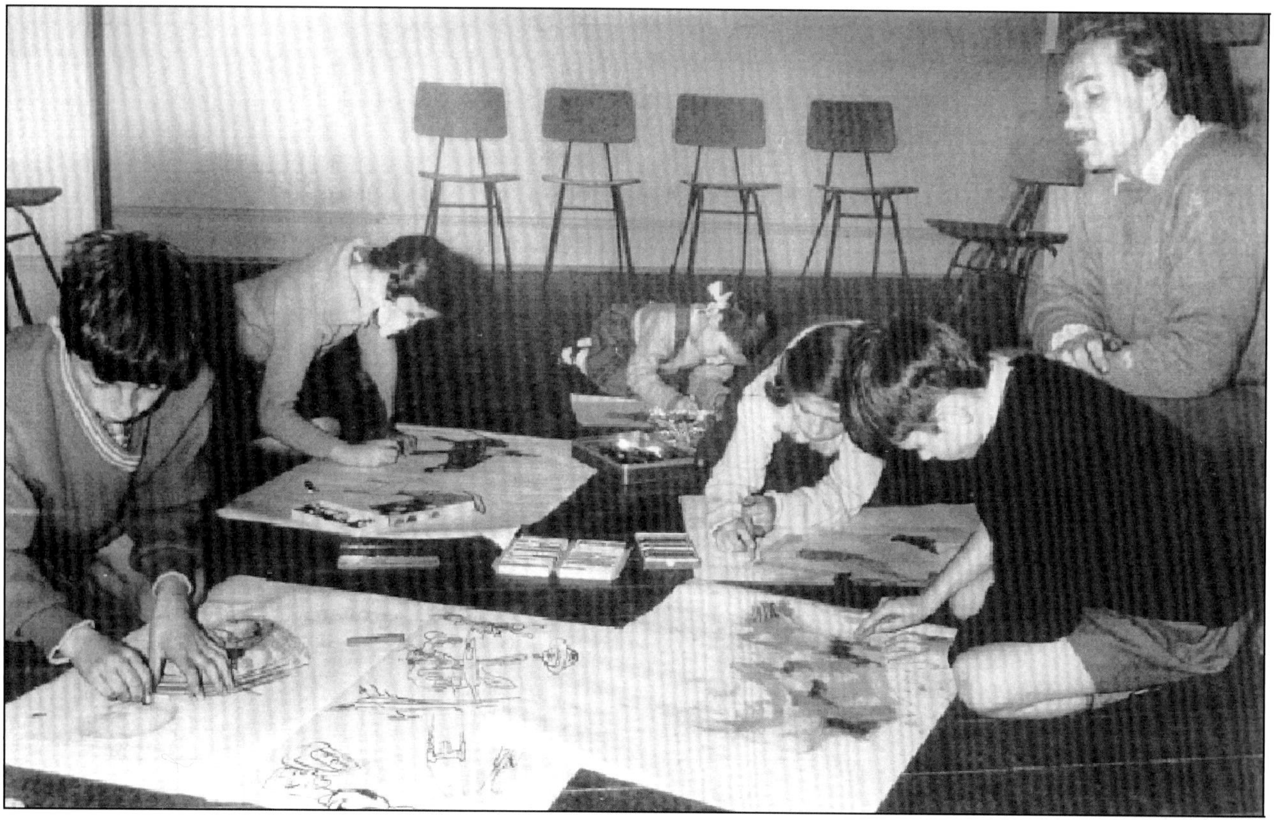

The Dutkiewicz children painting in the artist's studio: from left - Michal, Anna, Cecilia, Ursula and Adam - with their father, Wlad, overseeing. 1966, Adelaide. Photograph courtesy News Ltd.

John Bray

Preface

I am delighted to hear that a book is about to appear about Wladyslaw Dutkiewicz and I am honoured by being asked to introduce it.[1]

Wlad's life can be bisected into a European part before 1949 and an Australian part thereafter. The 24th August is a date of especial significance to him. On the 24th August 1939 the Hitler-Stalin pact providing amongst other things for a division of Poland between Germany and Russia came into operation. On the 24th August 1941 he fled from the Germans into the Ukraine. On the 24th August 1944 he was seized by the Nazis and transported to a concentration camp. On the 24th August 1949 he first set foot on Australian soil. And on the 24th August 1989, forty years later, in his seventies, he opened an exhibition that, in a sense, summed up his painting career.

He was an artist for all his adult life. He was trained in painting before the war at the Krakow academy in Poland and at the École des Beaux Arts in Paris. He studied at the Drama Academy of the National Theatre in Lwow and at the time of the outbreak of war in 1939 was its Assistant Director. This dual artistic attachment to painting and drama, which began in Europe, continued in a Polish Displaced Persons' camp in Bavaria and for years in Australia after it was over.

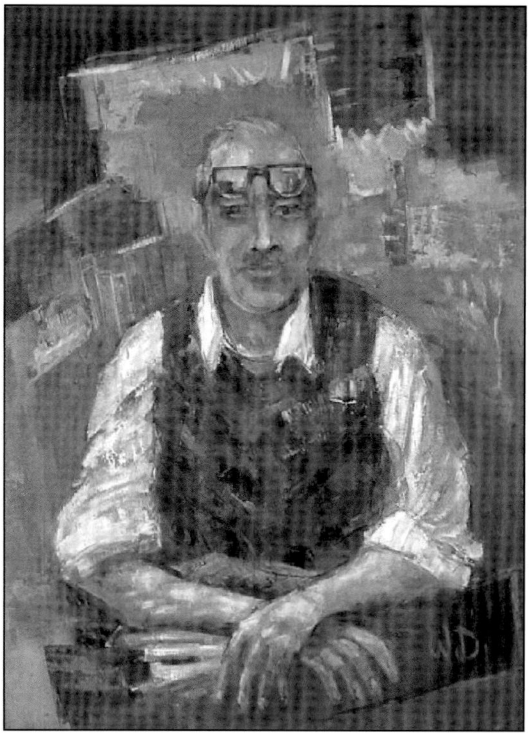

Wladyslaw Dutkiewicz. *South Australian poet (John Bray).* Oil on composition board. ca.1967, Adelaide. 122.0 x 90.5 cm. Gift of Don Dunstan 1987. Art Gallery of South Australia, Adelaide.

In Australia he had at first to paint in a somewhat utilitarian ambience. As he said to the press in 1953: "You know the Adelaide Railway Station? The platforms? The bright blue pillars and the bright blue roofs? I painted them. Picasso had his blue period. So did Dutkiewicz".[2]

But of course he never ceased to paint on canvas. His first exhibition in Adelaide was in 1951. Since then he exhibited widely in Adelaide but also in Melbourne, Sydney, Canberra, London and Canada. He won the Cornell Prize in 1951 and 1955 and was runner-up in 1953. In 1952 he won two silver medals at the Chamber of Manufactures' Royal Adelaide Exhibition and in 1956 he was joint winner of the Advertiser Prize Exhibition.

It would be tedious to enumerate a catalogue of exhibitions. As in Europe, so in Australia, he did not confine his artistic energies to painting, though painting was always his first love. He involved himself in the theatre, first as a stage designer, later as a producer. He formed a company of players, the Art Studio Players, and from 1959 to 1962 he introduced Adelaide audiences to Gorky and Wesker. He was prominent in the affairs of the Polish community. To name only one example in 1967 he produced a series of lively drawings, done backstage during the Melbourne season of a visiting Polish dance company.

I despair of enumerating all the activities of this many-sided man. I merely mention his appearance on television, in the course of which he broke his leg by falling off a six-foot wall, one of the colourful mishaps that have dotted his career.

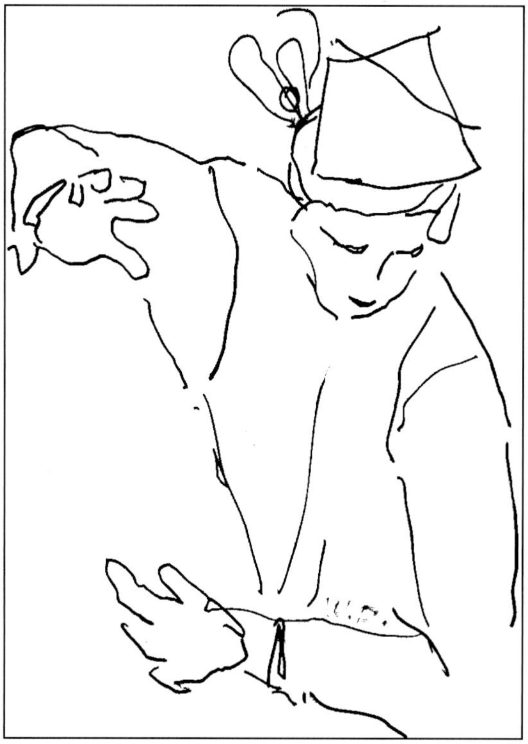

Wladyslaw Dutkiewicz. *Mazowsze* dancer. Felt pen on paper. ca.1967, Adelaide. 26.0 x 20.6 cm. Estate of the artist.

---

[1] Permission to reproduce remarks were included in a Typed Letter to the author, 24 January 1993. The preface is adapted from a Typed Speech, 24 August 1989, with minimal editorial changes required by circumstances and the passing of time. The completion of the manuscript was delayed by the author's other commitments.

[2] John Veitch, "Stalin doesn't like his paintings," *News*, 2 June 1952, 12.

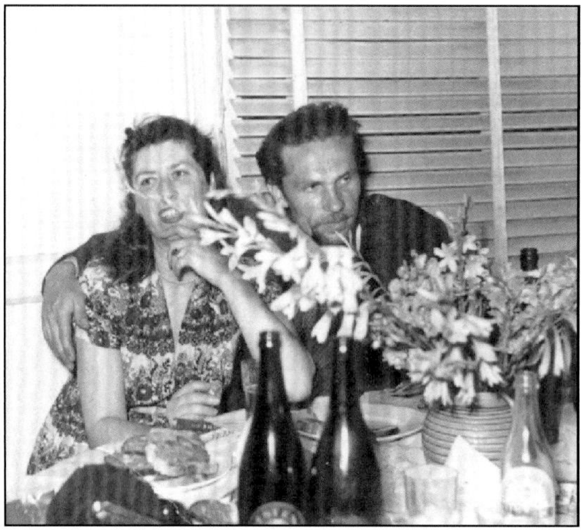

Wlad meets Joan. Photograph. 1950, Adelaide.

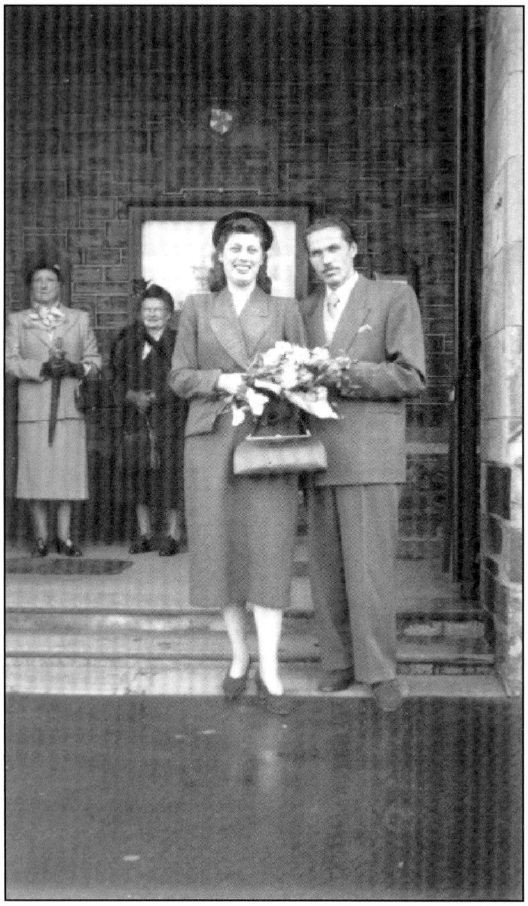

Wlad and Joan marry. 1953, Adelaide. Photograph by Cushla Doyle.

Wlad was not only an artist but an entertainer of artists. He and his devoted wife, Joan, presided for many years over a monthly salon in their house at Dulwich, attended by painters, actors, musicians, arts administrators and friends and patrons of the arts. Particularly notable were the New Year's Eve parties which used to begin a few hours before midnight and finish a few minutes after dawn, in time anyhow to reach the early morning bars which used to open in the 'fifties and 'sixties at 6am.

I have said enough, perhaps more than enough, about the man. Let us turn to the works. This book presents a survey of his art. It spans over fifty years of production. Wlad is primarily an abstract or expressionistic artist – I claim the layman's privilege of using technical terms loosely. In his manifesto in his 40th anniversary catalogue he explains and justifies abstract art, if it needs any justification, while freely admitting there are those who reject it. In this connection it is, I think, somewhat ironic that the critic of the *Manchester Guardian*, in discussing an exhibition in London by the Contemporary Arts Society of South Australia, says that the exhibition contains hardly anything for which the term "non-representational" really applies, although Wlad comes nearest to qualifying. But he adds: "even his well-arranged and agreeably coloured pictures turn out, on examination, to depict recognizable objects.[3]

I doubt whether he would say the same about all the pictures selected for reproduction here. Nevertheless the paintings here are by no means exclusively abstract. There are several representational works. In particular I refer to the drawings in which he catches ordinary people in postures and attitudes, which somehow encapsulate their personalities and their lives.

In 1974 Ivor Francis, then art critic of the Adelaide Advertiser, said: "Dutkiewicz's supreme importance as an original artist in his own right and as part of the texture of South Australian art is at last being recognized."[4] Art, like all human activities, is subject to time and the caprice of fashion, but I am sure that the recognition will endure despite passing shadows.

In short, Wlad is an artist of permanent achievement. In later years he suffered from ill-health and the inevitable vexations and deprivations of age. But this is no time to remember those things. He is a Renaissance man of manifold talents and multifarious activities. He has enriched the life of South Australia.

---

[3] Stephen Bone, *Manchester Guardian*, 9 August 1954.

[4] I. Francis, "Work of Polish-born artist is different," *Advertiser*, 3 July 1974, 18.

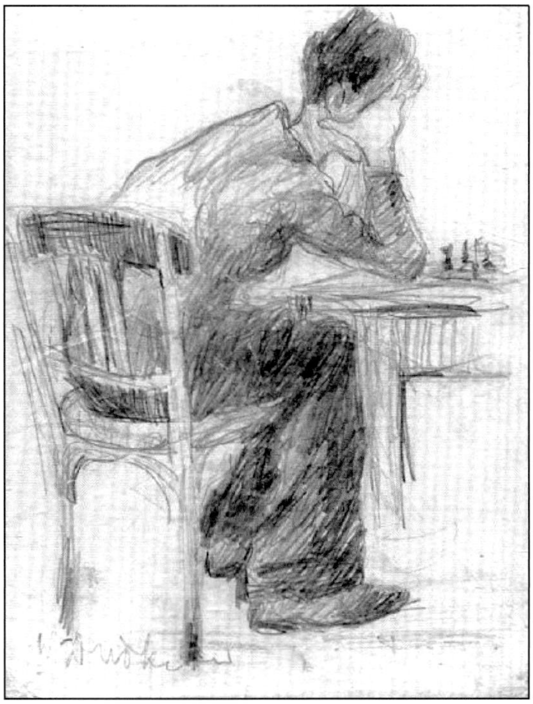

Chess player. Pencil on paper. ca.1946, Hohenfels, Germany. 19.5 x 15.2 cm. Dutkiewicz Archive.

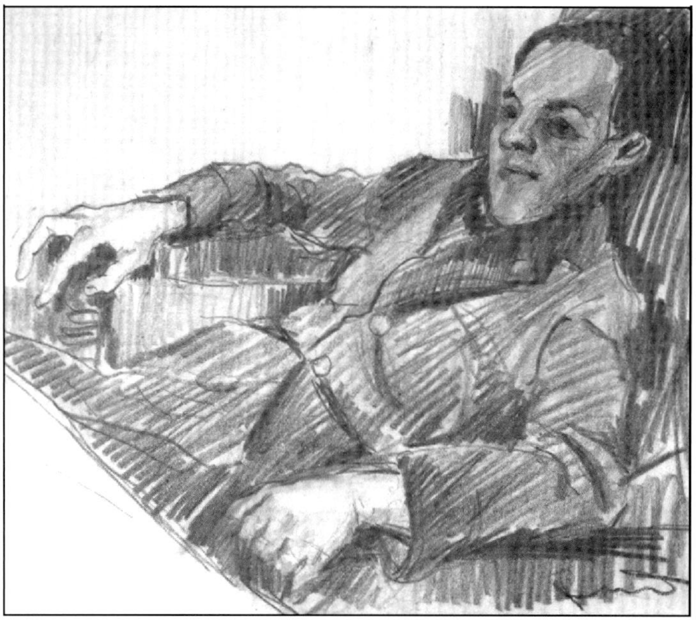

Sketch of Jan Dutkiewicz. Pencil on paper. ca. 1938, Krakow, Poland. 15.0 x 19.5 cm. Dutkiewicz Archive.

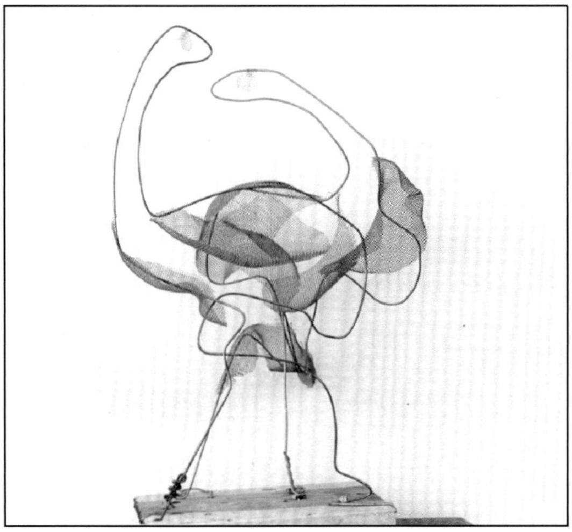

Emus. Architectural Convention Exhibition, Botanic Park. 1956, Adelaide. Steel rod, wire and wire gauze. approx. 180.0 x 150.0 x 80.0 cm. Estate of the artist. Photograph: Ian Davidson.

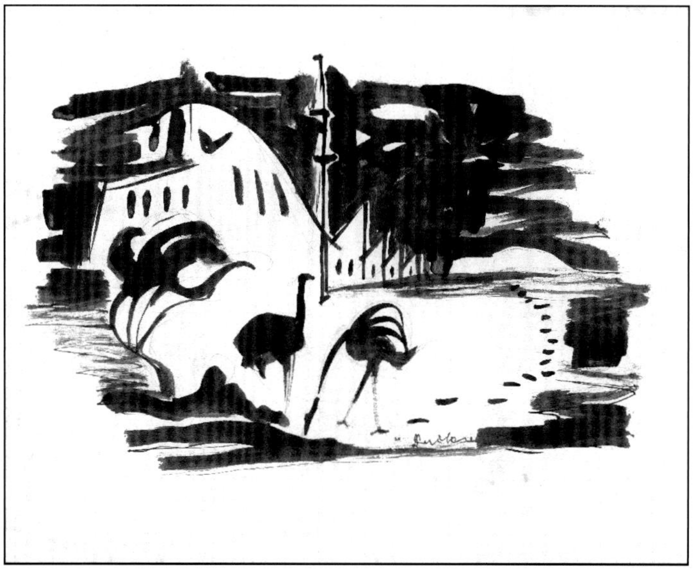

Emus and refugee barracks. Indian ink on paper. 1949, Northam, Western Australia. 20.0 x 25.0 cm. Dutkiewicz Archive.

Graphics, Sculptures and Public Art, 1938-68

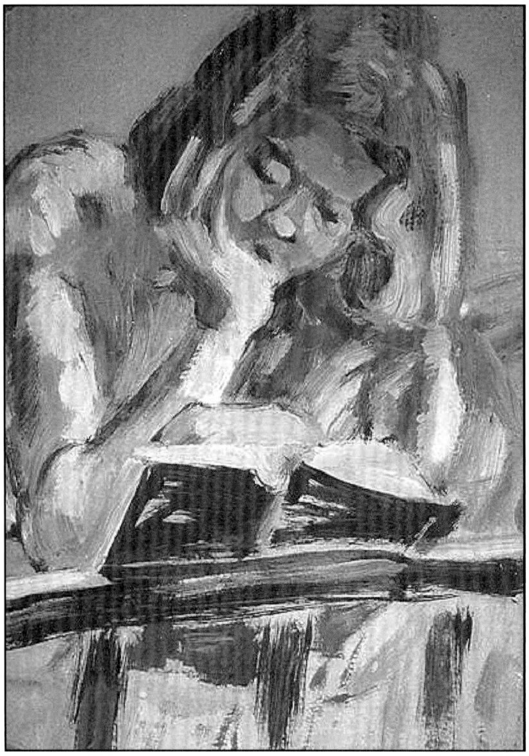

Girl reading. Model: Penelope Loveday. Oil on paper on board. ca.1950, Adelaide. 43.0 x 31.0 cm. Private collection, Perth.

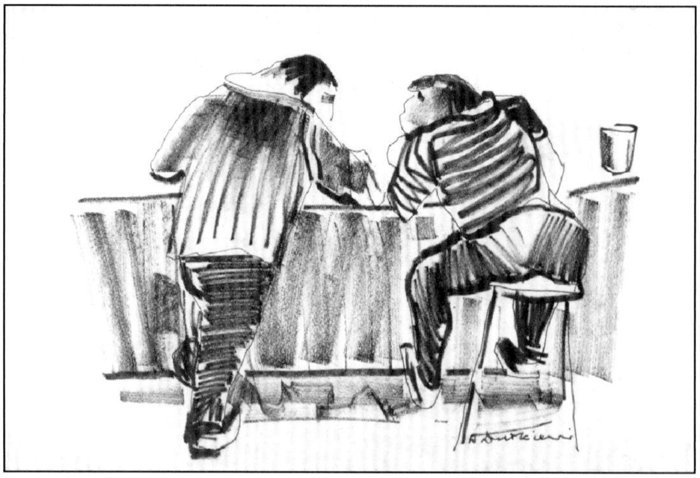

In the bar. Felt pen on paper. ca.1968, Adelaide. approx. 39.0 x 50.0 cm. Private collection, Adelaide.

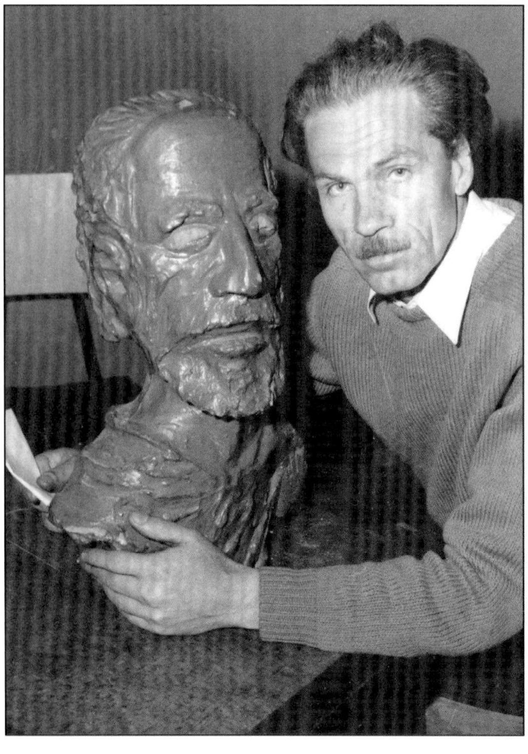

Wlad with his clay bust of Homer. Photograph. 1962, Adelaide. Photograph courtesy News Ltd. Dutkiewicz Archive.

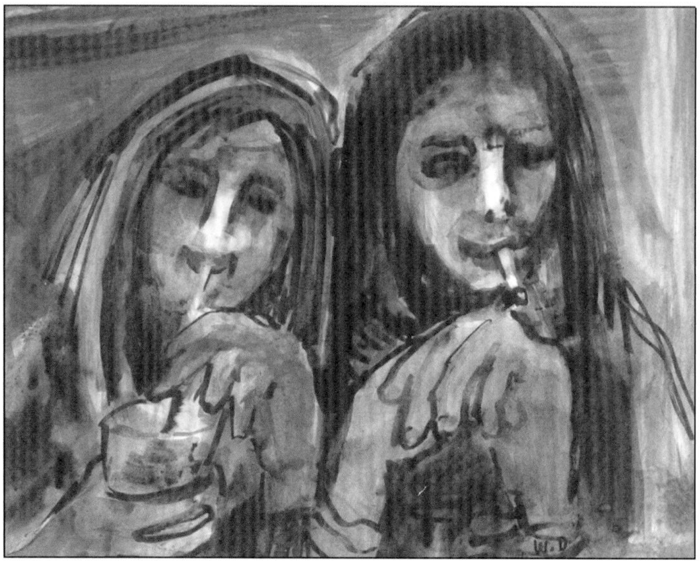

Beatniks. Felt pen, coloured inks on paper. ca.1967, Adelaide. 29.5 x 49.0 cm. Estate of the artist. Photograph: Graeme Hastwell.

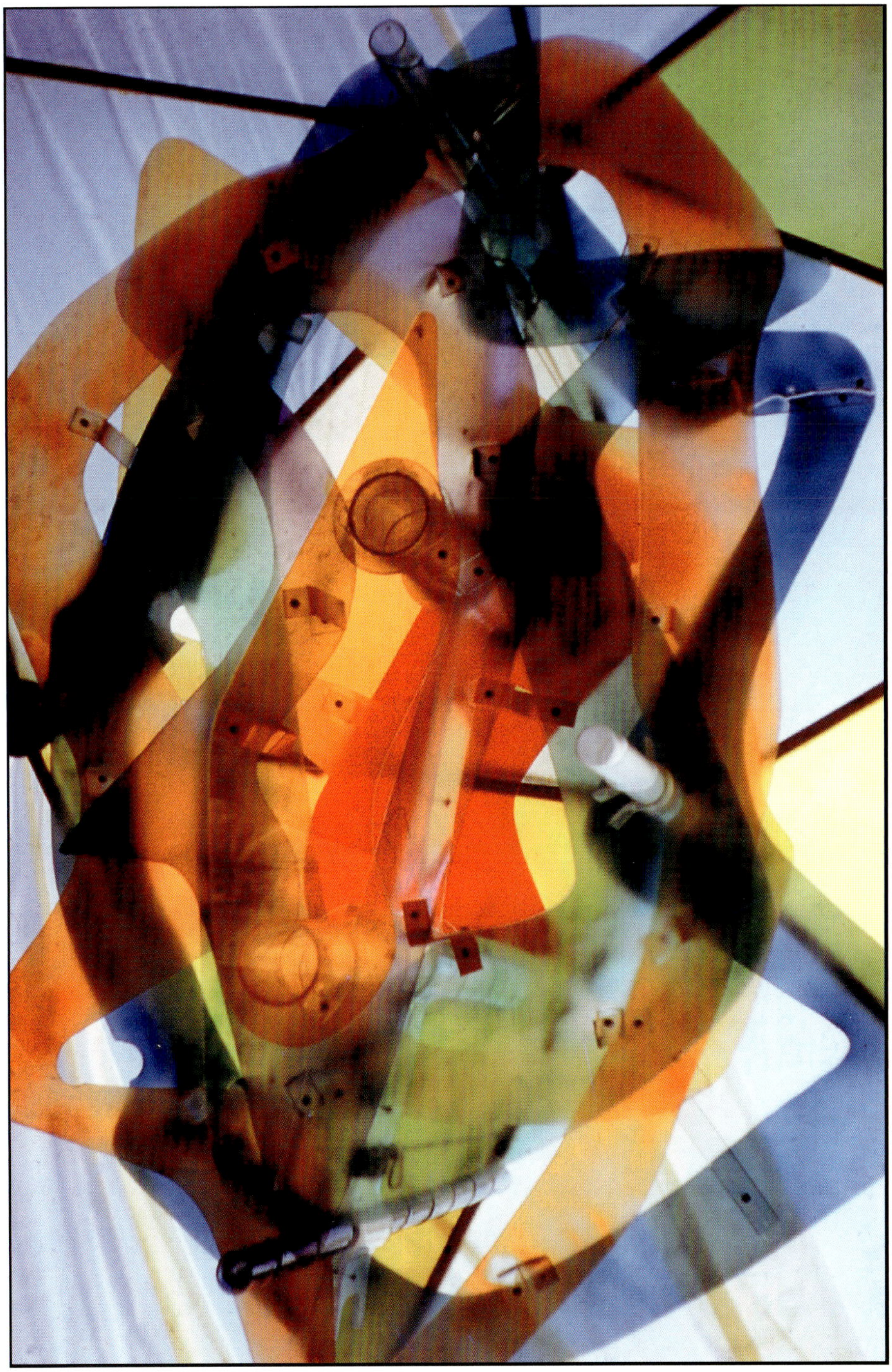

Mobile hanging sculpture. Coloured and clear perspex, wire and rivets.
Plastics Pavilion, Adelaide Architectural Exhibition, Botanic Park, June 1956.

This was a one-off piece Wlad later used as the basis for the steel rod and multi-coloured perspex street sculptures he designed for the 1968 Adelaide Festival of Arts. This work and those sculptures were a three-dimensional realization of his theory of "space-time painting", otherwise referred to as "Organic Constructivism"
(see Brian Claridge's explication starting on p. 49).

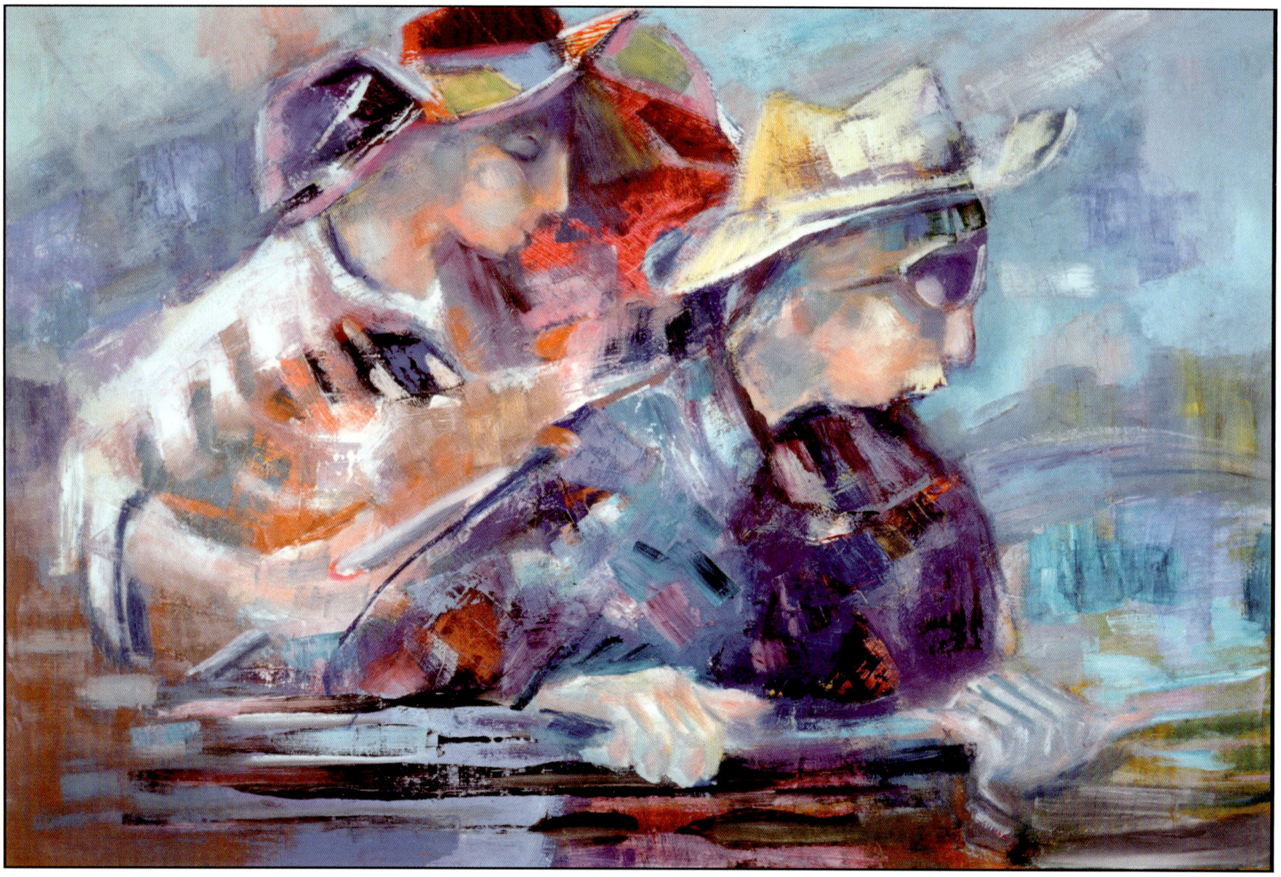

Fishing. Oil on composition board. ca.1970, Adelaide. 61.0 x 91.5 cm. Private collection, Adelaide. Photograph: Graeme Hastwell.

This is one of the most conventionally impressionistic canvases produced by the artist, underpinned by gentle observation and humour and beautifully conceived. I think Wlad used as models for the faces my older brother Michal, as the boy, and the man who used to mow the lawns at the family home. It was the one of the last paintings of a long line of work from ca.1964 depicting members of the growing family in a variety of poses and guises.

Selected Paintings 1968-1986

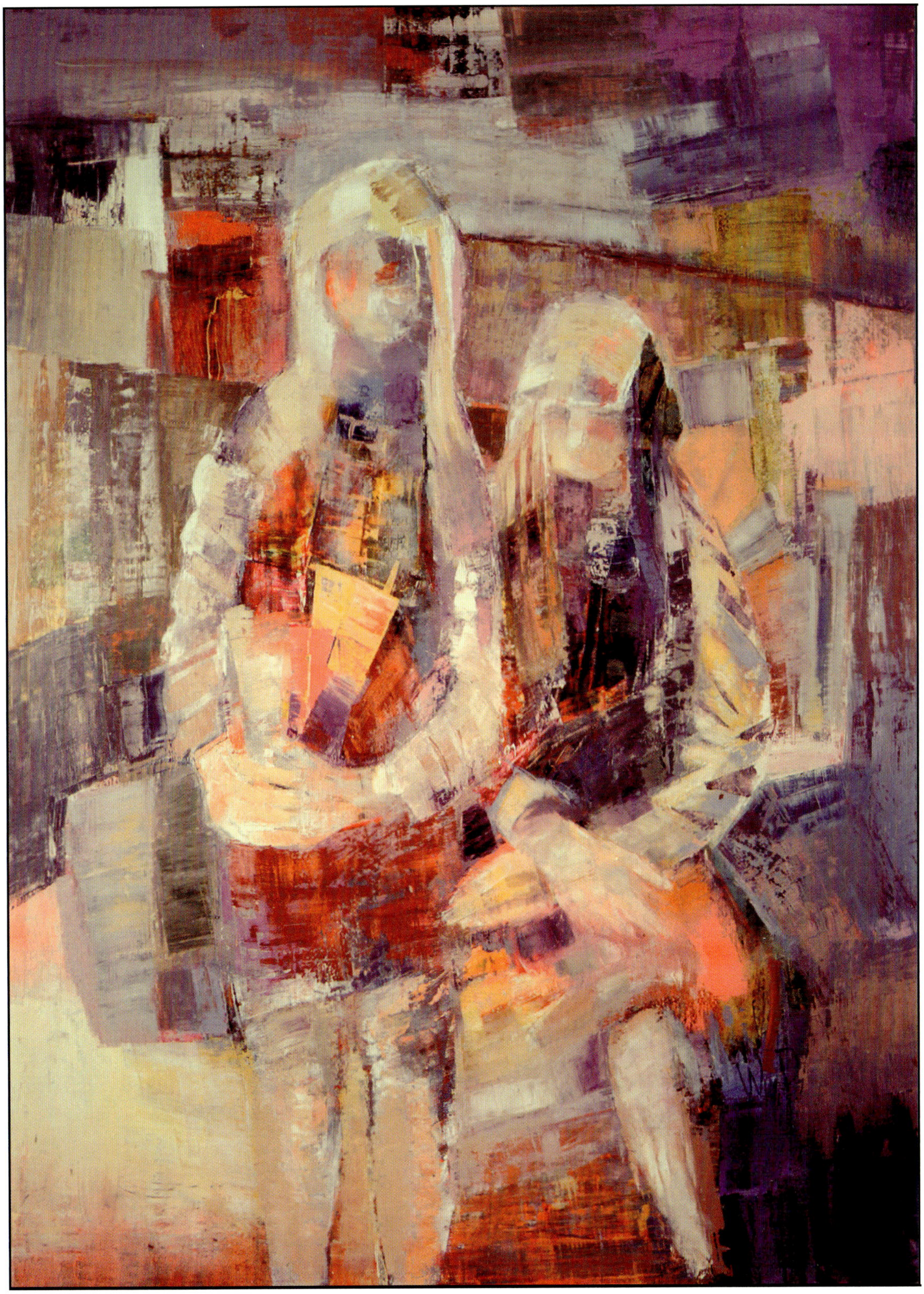

Sisters. Youth of Today series. Oil on composition board. 1968, Adelaide. 120.5 x 82.2 cm. Private collection, Adelaide. Photograph: Graeme Hastwell.

A beautiful painting with subtle colour and classical references, rendered with the artist's individual, modernist, palette-knife and scraper driven technique. Brushwork is used deftly and only occasionally for highlighting and softening.

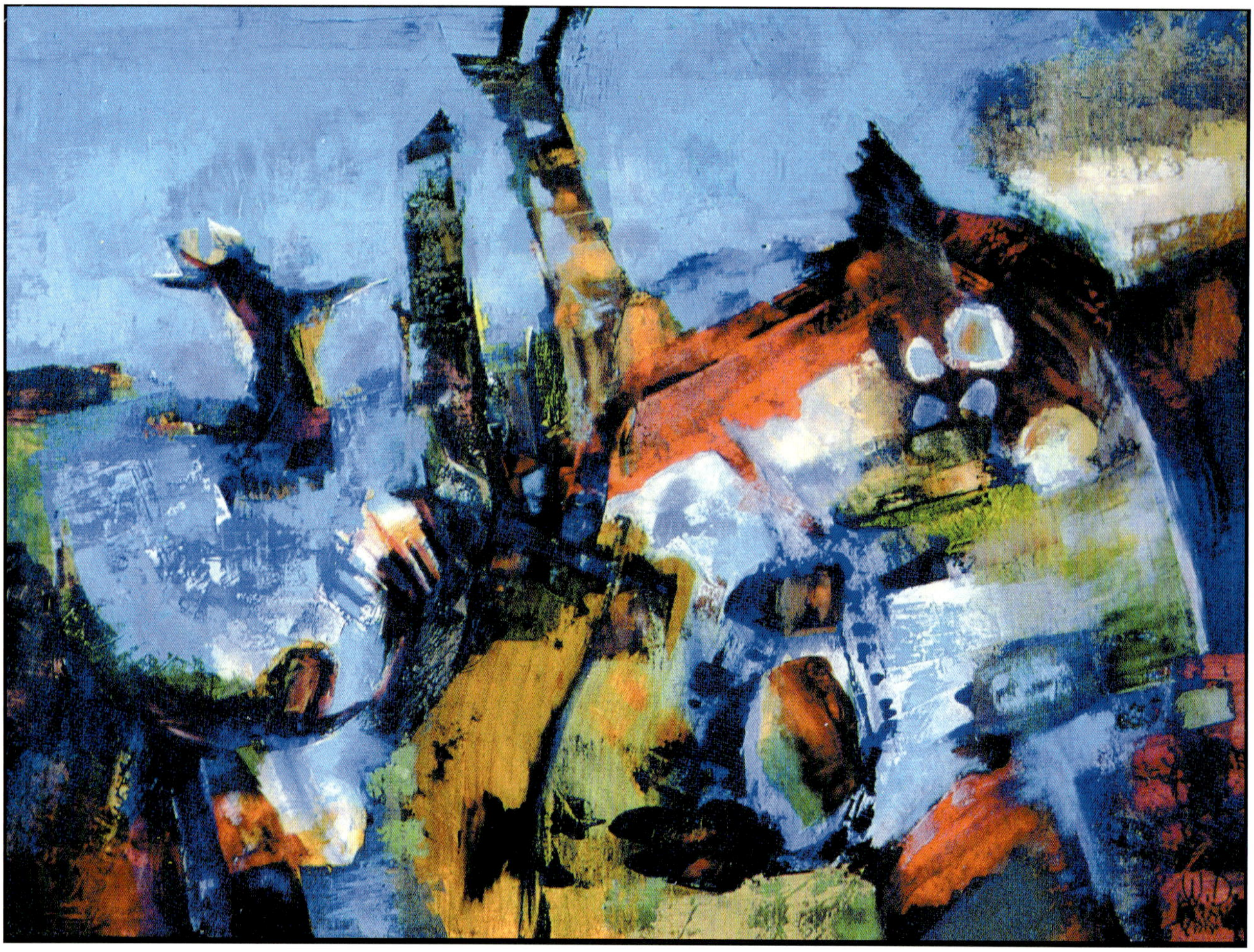

Blue Lake. Oil on composition board. 1972, Adelaide. 91.5 x 122.0 cm. National Collection/Artbank.

A visually poetic composition extrapolated from his conceptual starting point, the amazing limestone-tainted lake at Mt. Gambier in the south-east of South Australia. Wlad used an elevated and even aerial perspective for a number of his landscape-based paintings, beginning in the 1950s, in work such as *Wet Asphalt* and *City at Night* (p. 33). The intensity of the colour of the water is surprisingly true to life at the hottest time of year. Wlad painted several pictures in this vivid style, some sparse, like the predominantly white and grey *Snow*, and others more colourful and textured. The dark lines are created by using a particular roller with particular deftness. He began using this device in the early 1960s, mainly for imparting small details and textures, but gradually discovered more and more possibilities with it, until in this series he adopted it as the principle tool, overtaking the palette knives and scrapers he had utilised so much in the 1960s. Of course he continued to use brushes in paintings unless he felt they were not required at a conceptual level.

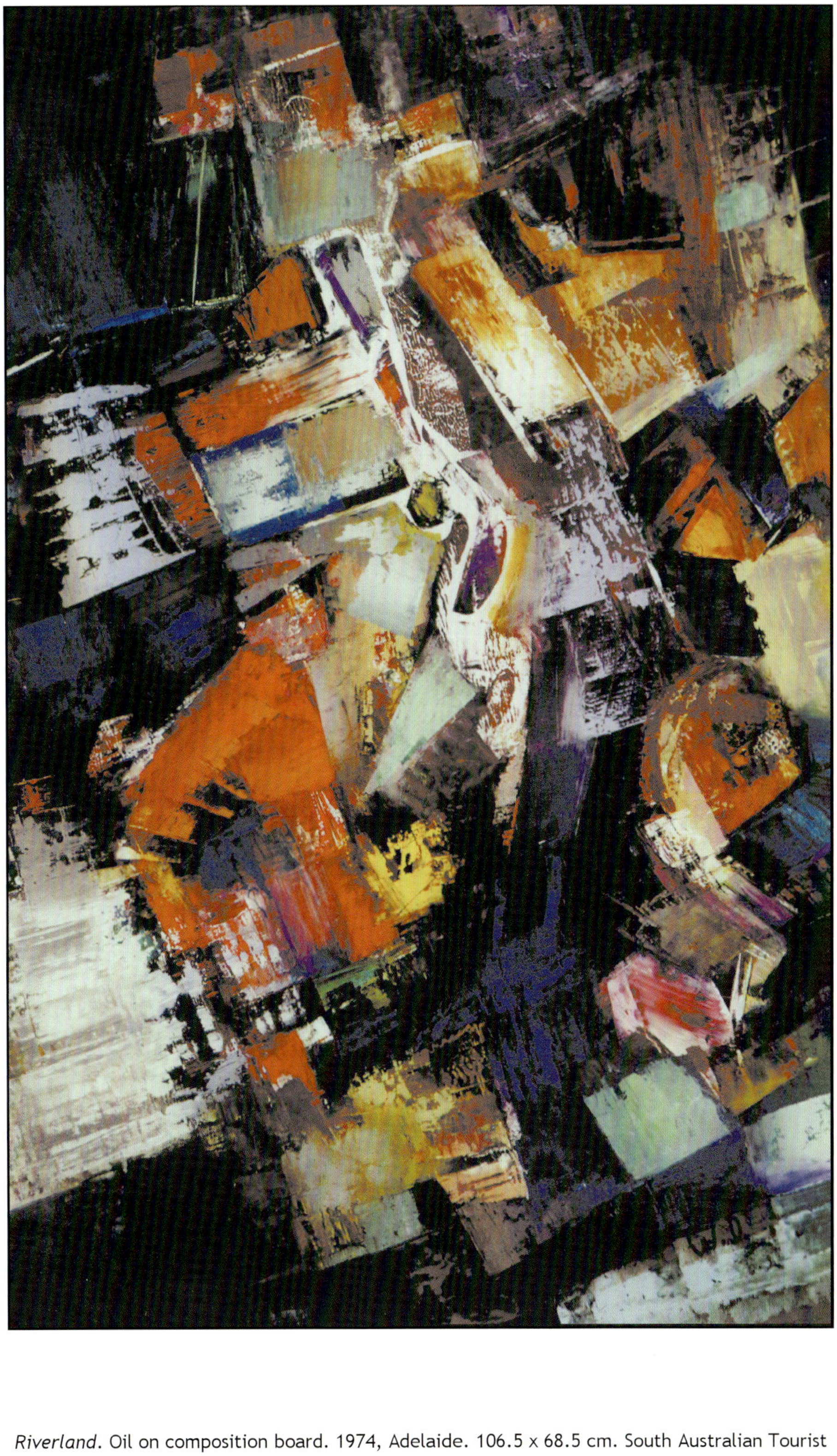

Riverland. Oil on composition board. 1974, Adelaide. 106.5 x 68.5 cm. South Australian Tourist Bureau. Photograph: Graeme Hastwell.

One of several works by local artists and photographers, including Jacqueline Hick, Robert Boynes and Jan Dalman, commissioned by the Bureau for a major promotional poster campaign.

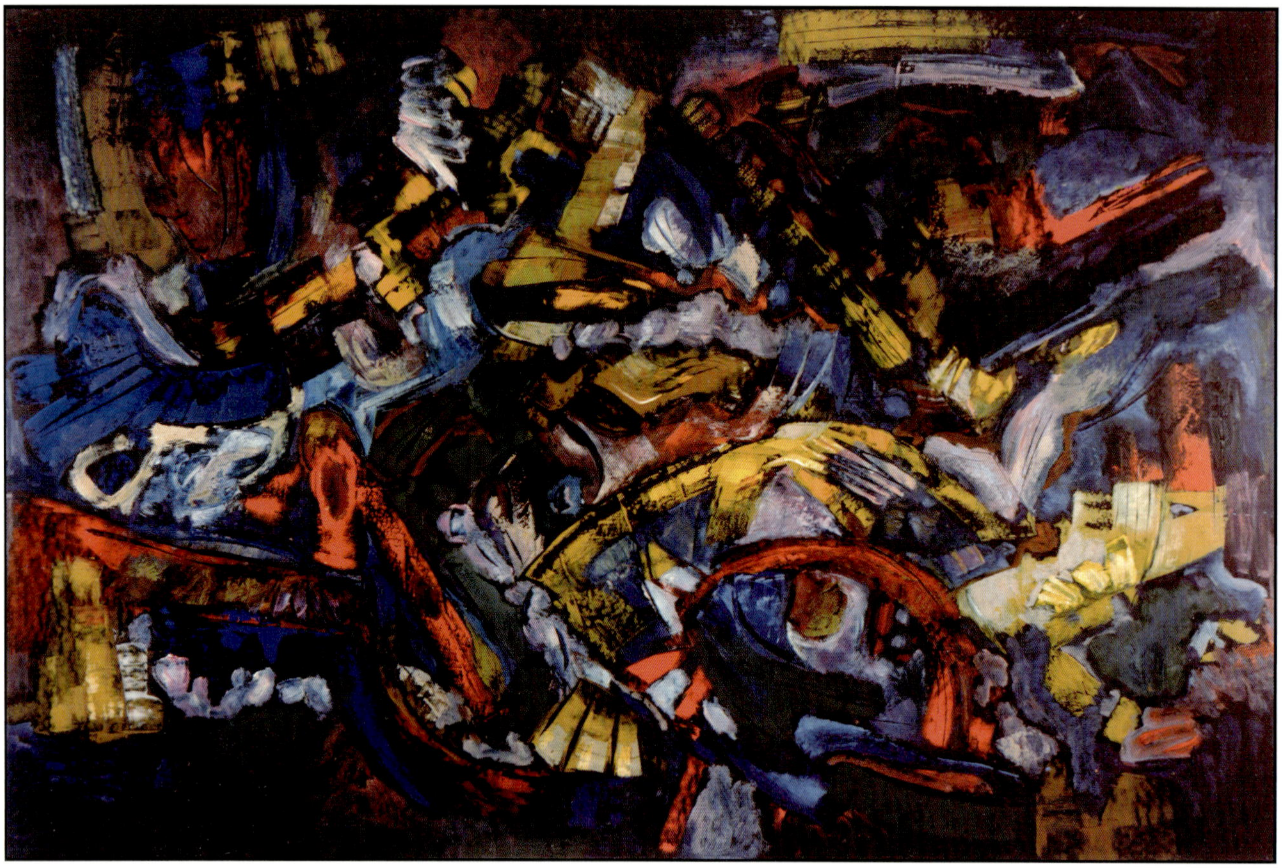

Night. Oil on composition board. 1976, Adelaide. 122.0 x 183.0 cm. Estate of the artist. Photograph: Graeme Hastwell.

Here Wlad operates in cosmic mode on a black background, connecting with elemental forces on a voyage into the summer night sky, with a meteor crashing through the Milky Way. The painting in style refers back to *Recluse* and *In Orbit* (p. 36), but it is treated with a more pyrotechnical, primary palette, predominantly based on permutations of ultramarine and cobalt blues, with reds and yellows used as highlights or toned back into the black, fused into tertiary shades of ochre, greens and greys.

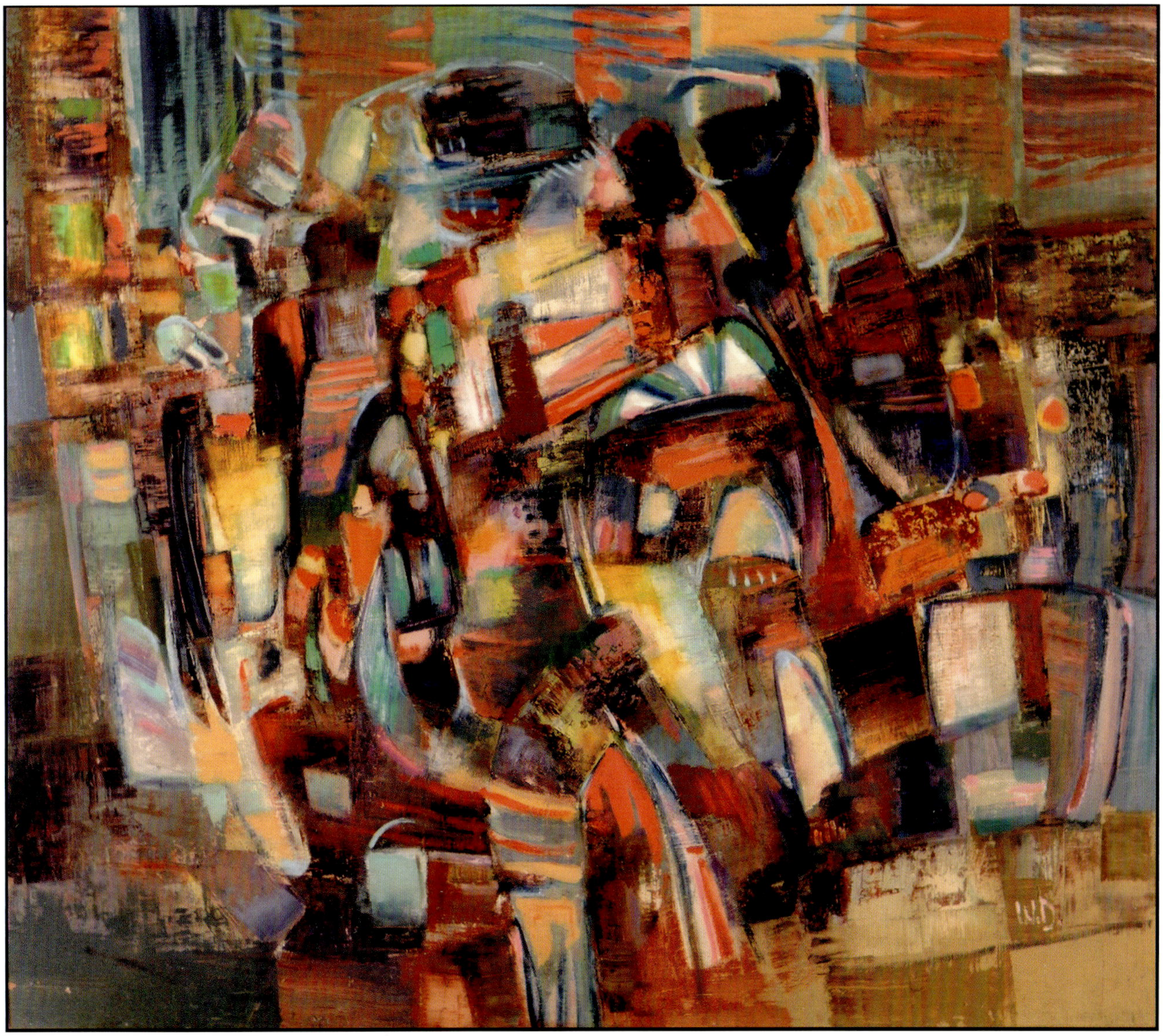

Flight out of Egypt. Oil on composition board. ca.1985, Adelaide. 122.0 x 137.0 cm. Estate of the artist.
Photograph: Graeme Hastwell.

One of the most sophisticated paintings by the artist, it is a variation on one of his favourite themes, "Refugees", but of Futurist inclination, with a view of figures from the front, not the more common aspect of the side, to indicate motion. The theme is also suggested by the rich orchestration of colours evocative of Northern Africa. An alternate title of *Pharaohs of Egypt* was used in the 1989 retrospective exhibition, but that did not indicate the reference to Exodus.

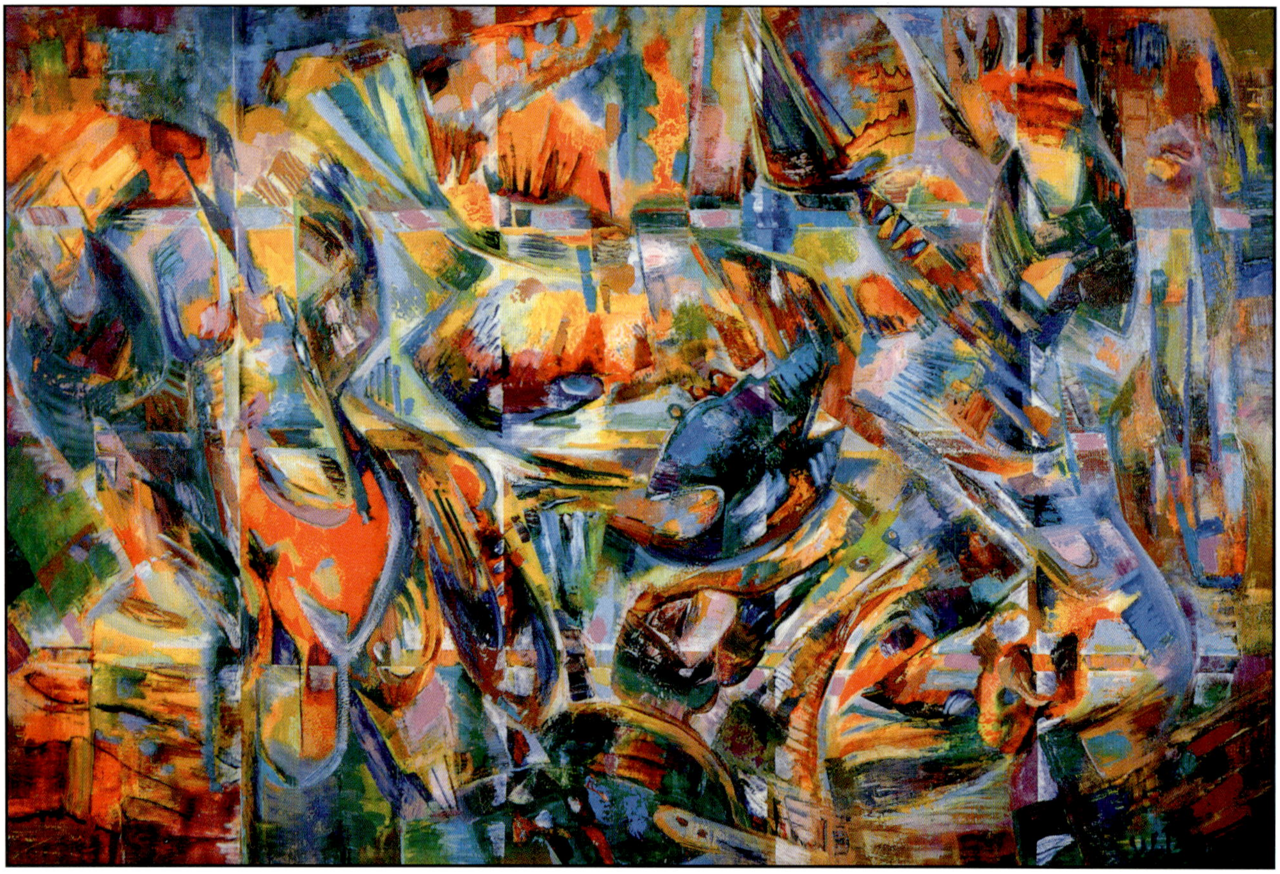

Twenty Centuries. Sesquicentenary/Bicentenary series. Oil on composition board. 1986-88, Adelaide. 122.0 x 183.0 cm. Estate of the artist. Photograph: Graeme Hastwell.

A remarkable painting that thematically returns to the massive and complex works of the mid 1950s, but based on the shapes developed for his street sculptures which were commissioned for the 1968 Adelaide Festival of Arts, situated on the median strip of King William Street in the centre of the city.

Truly one of his finest abstracts, and perhaps his greatest work from later years, it summarises many of the ideas and technical achievements of earlier periods. In this and other paintings from the series, he foregrounds a grid in the composition, an idea he had never worked with before. In a way it is a postmodern device that reveals and explains the internal workings and classical roots of his paintings: how he develops and integrates his composition over the entire picture surface so that each section has equal interest and value.

Adam Dutkiewicz

The Man with an Itch to Paint

One of the mysteries of life exists in the fact that each sibling has an entirely different relationship with each of their parents. In our family, in order of appearance, there was Michal (b. 1955), Adam (b. 1956), Ursula (b. 1958), Anna (b. 1959) and Cecilia (b. 1961). I think it is true to say that I knew my father best of the five children: my mother told me once I was the only one with whom Wlad really played. I remember as a toddler bouncing up and down on his knee in bed and laughing, as I quite often used to sleep with my parents. That joy translated across the years in my observation of his art and his theatre.

I did not know him at all before his motorcycle accident in 1956, and many people who did have told me I never knew him at his best. This includes his bravery and saving of many Polish, Jewish and Russian lives as a Polish partisan in the Second World War, and after it, the good deeds he did as leader of 16,000 Polish displaced persons and in fighting the repatriation of Poles to Stalinist Poland. At the same time he brought joy and laughter to many dispirited countrymen through his theatre troupe that toured the DP camps in Bavaria. No doubt he was haunted, like many soldiers, by things he had to do during the war. These stories of bravura and derring-do predate his appearance in Australia, when his painting became his dominant artistic practice, and, perhaps a little sadly, the means by which I most got to know my father.

I have few memories of times before 1962. I recall the house renovations in the early 1960s, which my father managed with architectural help from Brian Claridge and construction assistance from fellow migrant artist Anton Holzner and other theatrical workers, using funds from a settlement over the motorcycle accident. They built a large room for the children, a new bathroom and a painting studio. Around that time rehearsals for the Art Studio Players were held in the lounge-room in the front of the house, which was also modified. One of the troupe's patrons was Dr. John Bray, who later became Chief Justice and Chancellor of the University of Adelaide.

There was also an occasion, when I was in grade two at the local parish school, when the nun, having heard my father was an artist, asked if we could persuade him to make some drawings for the class. He was reluctant, being very busy at the time, but eventually produced a small selection of coloured felt pen drawings showing children in raincoats sloshing through puddles (later, he developed it into an oil painting). The drawings were delightful, yet when I presented them to the nun, she blurted "I thought you said your father was an artist!" That reaction ultimately spelt the end of our presence in the school, after more than a year, but I was later told that despite the nun's initial disapproval, he was asked to paint the sets for the school plays, which he did without my knowledge.

There was also the regular excitement of the monthly parties, especially from around the time that The Beatles' *Love Me Do*, *Please Please Me* and *Norwegian Wood* were hits. Most intimate of all, I remember a day, a few years later, when Wlad arranged for me to have a day off school to go to see Marcel Marceau, whom he claimed he knew in Paris before the war.

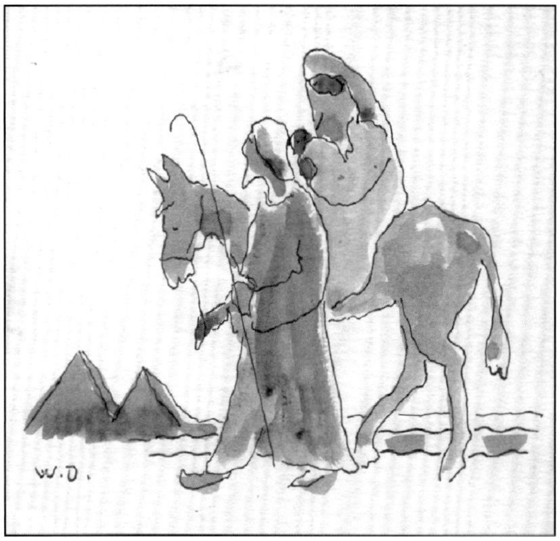

Joseph, Mary and the infant Christ. Hand-coloured printed card. ca.1951, Adelaide. 11.5 x 12.5 cm. Dutkiewicz Archive.

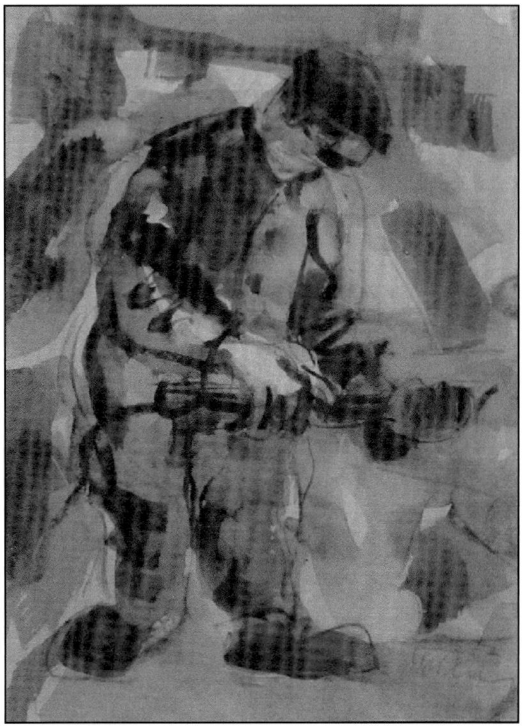

Driller. Pencil & watercolour on paper. ca.1952, Adelaide. 29.0 x 21.5 cm. Private collection, Adelaide. Photograph: Graeme Hastwell.

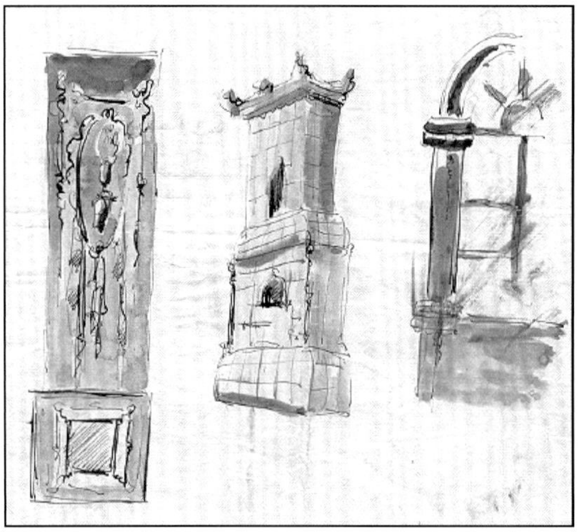

Sketch for set design, *A Man must live*. Pencil, pen & sepia wash on paper. 1950, Adelaide, Dutkiewicz Archive.

What remained in my mind was not so much the performance, which was mesmerising and magical, but the magnificent painting of the mime artist Wlad produced subsequently. Its whereabouts are now unknown: unfortunately, I have been unable to trace the painting, only two drawings.

In the same year, 1967, I remember being absolutely enchanted by my father's production of Henrik Ibsen's *The Wild Duck* for the Adelaide University Theatre Guild (p. 20). The tenderness of gesture and sensitivity of the theatrical imagery awoke in me an understanding of Wlad's vision, which I gleaned was profoundly original in its emotional underpinning and rhythm.

These two experiences were pivotal in our relationship. They ignited in me some kind of interest in understanding his mind, something I began to take seriously in 1986, when I began to interview and talk to him for my biography. It was a connection never shared with the other siblings, who had not left home as young as me and remained closer to the family home. They had not been brought so closely into his world, and were more thoroughly exposed to his personal and fatherly failings as he aged: the overwhelming selfish, anti-social and even self-destructive aspects of his personality.

In many respects, however, Wlad's character was like the time of his death in Adelaide, on Saturday morning, 2 October 1999, when a rolling, rumbling storm with flashes of illumination passed through the city. Storms are rare in Adelaide, but on this occasion I sensed a disquiet, and could not fail to observe those flashes of brilliance were many and often spectacular. Not long after his death, I was waiting for a bus on The Parade, with tears streaming down my face, looking at the rain and the water washing away in the gutters. As the thunder rumbled across the plains towards the hills and disappeared, it felt like his soul was being taken with the storm, the claps of thunder reminding me of his voice in childhood times in moments of aggression and admonishment.

From my research into his art it is clear that initially he was not too experimental: the paintings he managed to execute in Bavaria after the war were solid yet quite tame exercises in landscape, still-life and portraiture, in which he searched to find his "voice". They were produced in a well-crafted, rather academic style, but showed flair with brushwork and a finely tuned sensibility and flair for expression and abstraction.

His early painting in Australia, however, indicates an amazing and torrential outpouring of pent-up creative energy. Wlad's first solo exhibition was at Curzon Gallery in early June 1951. The work caused a sensation among the circles of artists and exhibition-goers. During his first solo shows at the Royal South Australian Society of Arts patrons were seen queuing up the stairs and outside of the Institute Building on North Terrace waiting for the gallery to open.

The enormous and wide-reaching impact Wlad had on the art world in Adelaide extended beyond visual arts. The research undertaken on the Adelaide theatre scene in the exhibition *A Brush with the Stage* (1992) fully revealed to me his experience in theatre, both in Hohenfels in Germany and in Adelaide. We discovered, for instance, that he had retained his concept sketch for a set for the opera *La Traviata*, which he had prepared in post-war Germany, and exhibited it in his first major exhibition in Australia in 1951.

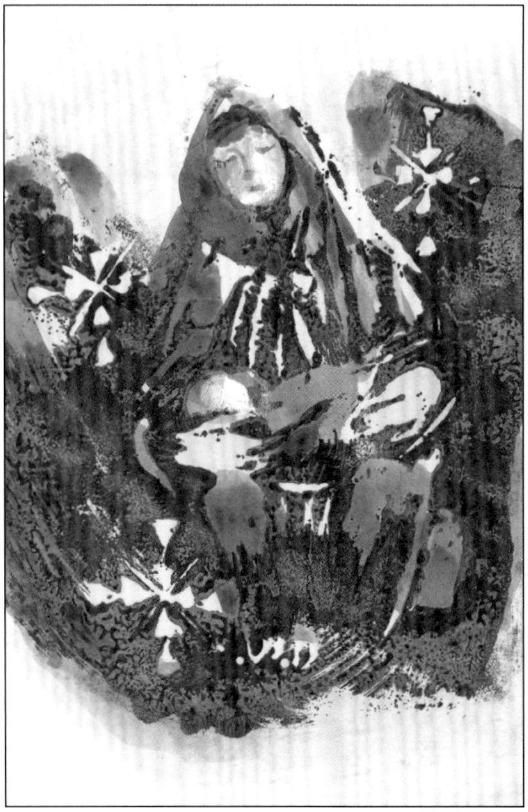

Madonna and child. Hand-coloured linocut. ca.1964, Adelaide. 19.0 x 12.5 cm. Dutkiewicz Archive.

It was a surprise to find that his sepia-coloured, daguerreotype-like sets for Francis Flannagan's production of Alexander Ostrovsky's *A Man Must Live* (previous page), in November 1950, were his first achievements to catch the eyes of critics in Australia. Soon after he was commissioned to design sets for Iris Hart's production of Federico Garcia Lorca's *The House of Bernarda Alba* (1951) and again for Flannagan's interpretation of Ivan Turgenev's *A Month in the Country* (1952).

While recovering from his accident in 1957, he collaborated with Thomas Steel on the set designs for John Edmund's productions of *Fallen Angels* and *Bus Stop*. My mother recalled he also collaborated with Jacqueline Hick on *Anna Karenina* in 1959.

In painting, his exploration of modernist styles and his personal synthesis of them, in his first six years in Adelaide, were truly revolutionary, especially in the context of Australian art of the period. This was duly noted by a number of people attuned to contemporary art, most notably Max Harris and Ivor Francis, who wrote glowing reports on this "New Australian" artist and the stunning impact he was having on the local art scene. Within a year Lisette Kohlhagen and Dorrit Black, before her death in 1951, were also heaping praise on Wlad while the conservative reviewers were horrified.

The debate about radical modernism in Adelaide was reignited well before the *French Painting Today* touring exhibition in 1953, an event often highlighted as a turning point in Australian art, as it heralded the rise of abstract painting, which Wlad regarded as an art of limitless possibilities.

Douglas Roberts, the well-known surrealist and expressionist painter and later Head of the South Australian School of Art, in reviewing Wlad's watercolour exhibition in 1952, made a Dave Dallwitz-like rhyming pun with the artist's name when he referred to the artist's "itchy brush".[5] Several years on Dallwitz himself, in his effervescent verbal style, referred to Wlad's imaginative art as "Dutkiewitchery".[6]

Wlad had won the Cornell Prize at the CAS on its inaugural occasion in 1951 and again in 1955; in the intermediate years he won several medals and prizes. He was one of seven artists featured in the film *Painting 1950-1955 South Australia*, selected by his peers at the Contemporary Art Society of South Australia.

Wlad was regarded as a pioneer of experimental modernism not only in Adelaide but also in the eastern states. His artistic output was multi-faceted: initially it was mainly driven by Expressionism, but it also forced its way into the abstract. There was also a fusion of meta-geometrical and expressionist approaches that was unique in Australian art. Instead of remaining fixed to a formal geometrical structure (traceable from Cézanne's theories back to Platonic classicism), Wlad tended to pursue an interest in automatist line and organic, Euclidian (spatial) geometrical and fourth-geometrical form.

In my thesis, following terms used in a manifesto, written by Brian Claridge but modelled on my father's theories (p. 49), I referred to this Adelaidian version of Ralph Balson's and Grace Crowley's Constructivist project in Sydney, dating from the 1940s, as "Organic Constructivism."

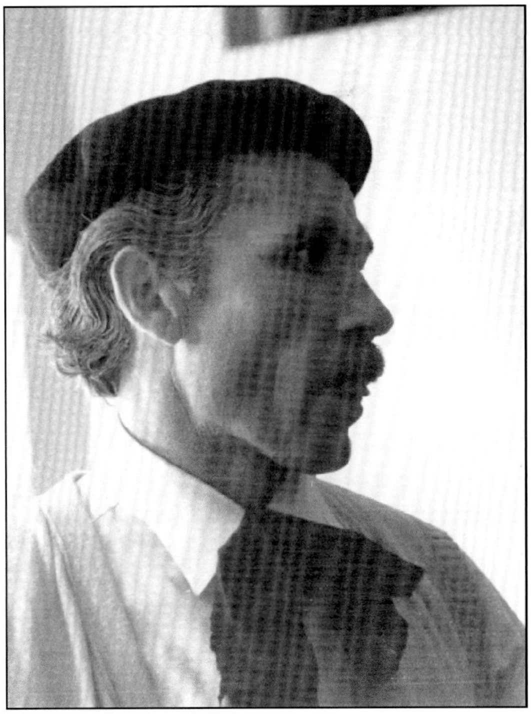

John Walpole. Wladyslaw Dutkiewicz backstage during *The Unquiet Spirit*. Black and white photographic print. 1959, Adelaide. Dutkiewicz Archive.

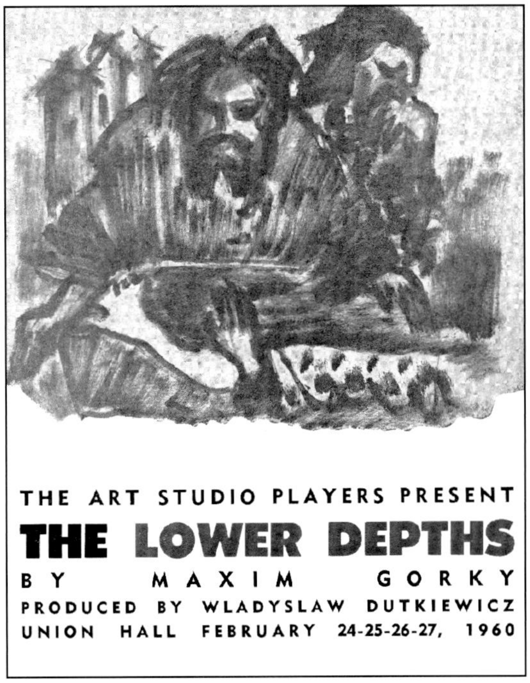

Programme, *The Lower Depths*, with brush drawing by W. Dutkiewicz. 1960, Adelaide. Dutkiewicz Archive.

---

[5] D. Roberts, "A Dut takes to water," for *Mary's Own Paper*, ca. June 1952, unpaginated.

[6] D. Dallwitz, *Ivor's Art Review* 1, no. 9, July 1957, 18.

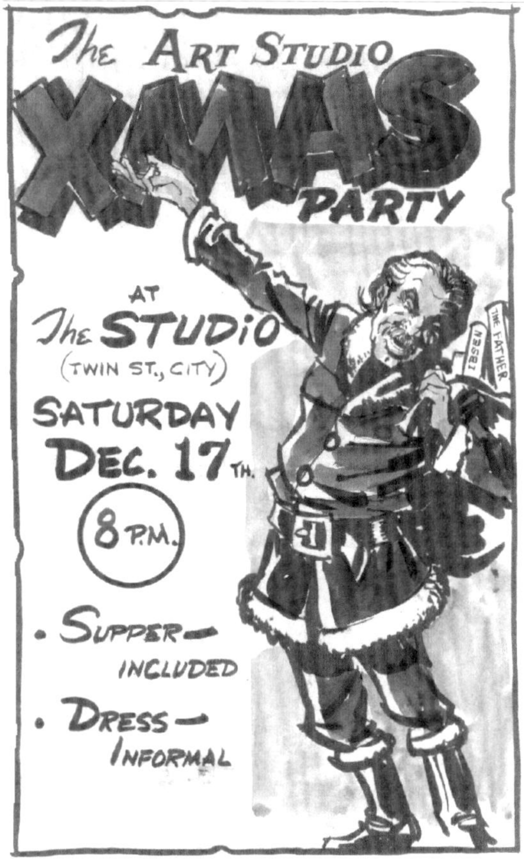

L. Dutkiewicz. Invitation to Christmas Party, Art Studio Players, Twin Street. 1961, Adelaide. Private collection, Adelaide. Photocopied for Dutkiewicz Archive.

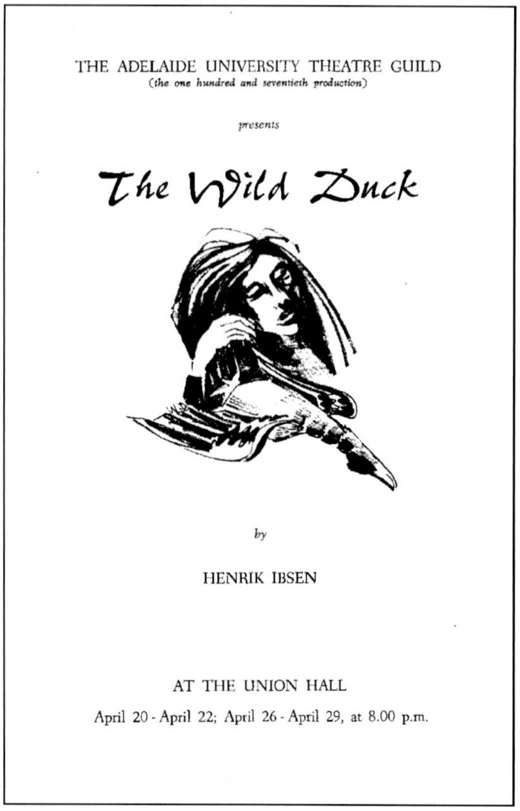

Programme for *The Wild Duck*. Felt pen drawing by W. Dutkiewicz. 1967, Adelaide. Dutkiewicz Archive.

The head injuries in the motorcycle accident forced Wlad to temporarily abandon painting in late 1956. He lost his memory and was colour blind, and had several operations to correct problems in his skull. In the process of reclaiming his memory he turned to his theatrical training and Constantin Stanislavsky's Method, in which he was schooled before the war in Poland.

Thespian visitors to the house noted Wlad's text books and activities, and because the Method was all the rage, began to ask questions. When he was sufficiently recovered, he was asked to produce a play for the Adelaide University Theatre Guild, and his unusual and spare production of Jean Jacques Bernard's *The Unquiet Spirit* aroused greater interest.

He formed a new troupe, the Art Studio Players, to explore the Method and his own ideas on theatre. He produced several challenging plays, including works by Maxim Gorky (*The Lower Depths*), Henrik Ibsen (*The Master Builder*, *The Father*), Arthur Miller (*All my Sons*), Arnold Wesker (*Roots*) and Bernard Kops (*The Dream of Peter Mann*). The first and latter two were Australian premières.

When he returned to painting, gradually but with utter conviction in 1960, his art moved towards a mature phase, not only abstract but also a highly personalised stylistic interpretation of the human figure, informed by his work in the theatre. He produced drawings and paintings on an earlier theme, his contact with Aborigines in Western Australia in 1949, and depicted in his highly personalised style the touring Bolshoi and Mazowsze ballet companies, his own theatre group and the parties, the street performers in the Festival, the Russian circus and the Adelaide Christmas Pageant. He also painted fleeting moments in life that he was able to somehow photograph in his mind and develop into superbly coloured and textured, poetic encapsulations of experience.

The most tender of these concerned his children in everyday circumstances, such as playing with toys, hanging out together or eating ice creams. On one occasion he painted my oldest sister, Ursula, and a friend, Radha Claridge, sitting at the feet of local artistic bohemian Francis Roy Thompson. In only one of these paintings, *Children playing*, did my father depict me, with yellow pallor, a reference not only to my litany of illnesses as a child but also to his initial memory of me, as I was born with jaundice. He did, however, produce at least one drawing or painting about each of his children, such as the bold and expressive felt pen drawings of my older brother, Michal, reading comics, and me, painting on the floor. There were also the gentle and amusing caricature *Ursula's toy* (ca.1962) (p. 39), which was produced in two versions, and *Backyard* (ca.1970), in which he depicts Cecilia hanging up the washing with Lisa Claridge.

Wlad's figurative painting was delightful: it had a comic edge and was unconventional, often rendered with scrapers then highlighted or softened with brushwork. He moved this technique further towards the abstract on numerous occasions, as in the dynamic semi-abstract *Youth Orchestra* (ca.1964), *Sisters* (p. 9), *Protest* (1968) (p. 44) and *School crossing*, based on the drawings he made for the nun several years earlier.

We remember him supervising us as children in a group, sometimes painting on the floor of the lounge-room, which by then he used as his studio, having forfeited the new room for the boys' bedroom. He worked in long bouts of tactical contemplation; we often quietly and considerately tiptoed past, the exploded into excited energy as we found ourselves in the bottom of the house.

Wlad's engagement with life was total: he was in everything, from high art and theatre to the Anzac Day march, the bars, the races, the landscape, the Asian markets, and even among the outcasts living on the streets. He painted in his highly individual and pyrotechnical style these themes and schoolgirls, refugees, beatniks, demonstrators, politicians, opal miners, shoppers, building site workers, footballers and cricketers, the nudes on Maslins Beach, Hare Krishnas, Buddhist icons, Madonnas, nuns, saints, Christ and the crucifixion, and the Pope.

He depicted places such as Monte Cassino in Italy, the Warsaw ghetto, the South Australian museum, the local zoological and botanical gardens, as well as office towers, imagined cities in far off-places, and promoted the science-fictional possibility of inhabiting Antarctica. He painted the *Sputnik* in orbit (p. 35), bull-dozers, emus and bird-life, cattle and horses, the storms, floods, bushfires, dams and salt pans, the unique landscapes of the Blue Lake (p. 11) and Tower Hill (p. 48), and further afield, the Snowy Mountains.

He ventured in his imagination to Mexico, the volcanic disasters of Mt. Lamington in Papua New Guinea and Mt. Pinatubo in the Philippines, and retuned via his memory to Poland, to the war and his experiences in exile in Europe. He painted and drew about current affairs, such as the *Voyager* disaster, the Vietnam War and Pol Pot. I can only hint at the scope of his work in the small selection I have included here.

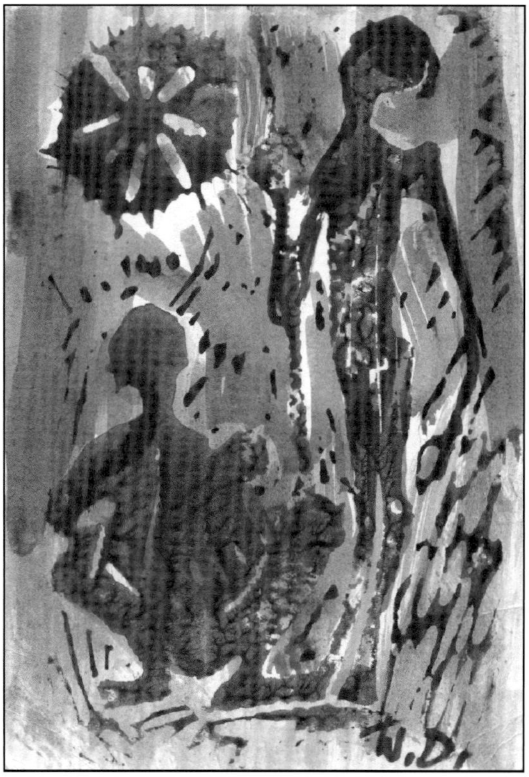

Hunters. Hand-coloured linoprint on card. 1962, Adelaide. 18.0 x 12.4 cm. Dutkiewicz Archive.

On one occasion, when I was almost a teenager, he took me to visit a house in a neighbouring street in Dulwich, where a group of Polish refugees were living as vagabonds, drunk and dispossessed. Wlad straight away took all the money from his pockets and gave it to them; he saw that one of them had no jacket, and it was the middle of winter, so he took off his own and gave it to him. That moment revealed to me not only Wlad's generosity but his conception of his future; I recall him telling my mother (in 1968 I think, when he was fifty) he had used up all his luck and was now destined for a "black fate." I think he knew that he was an artist who had fallen into the gap between two cultures. He was never really seen as an Australian artist.

Those comments marked the beginning of difficult times, as he began to drink far too much and close himself off from family life. The extension of hotel opening hours suited him well. But through the ensuing years Wlad's brilliance as an artist shone and he maintained his integrity of vision. Until 1976, he produced many wonderful paintings, of astonishing intensity and crystallised lucidity, that will remain with me forever. Somehow he was still able to achieve magnificent results in significant and often large, geometrically and otherwise complex works until the late 'eighties, and on rare moments since then in simpler formats, despite his declining eyesight and health.

In the early 1960s Wlad wrote for one of his WEA lecture series: "A work of art is not often recognisable when it is newly born: by definition it eludes all conventional ideas of what it ought to be. Art is a creation which offers no guarantees. The artist is a person walking into space, and we cannot know by what miracle the solid earth rises up to support his feet."

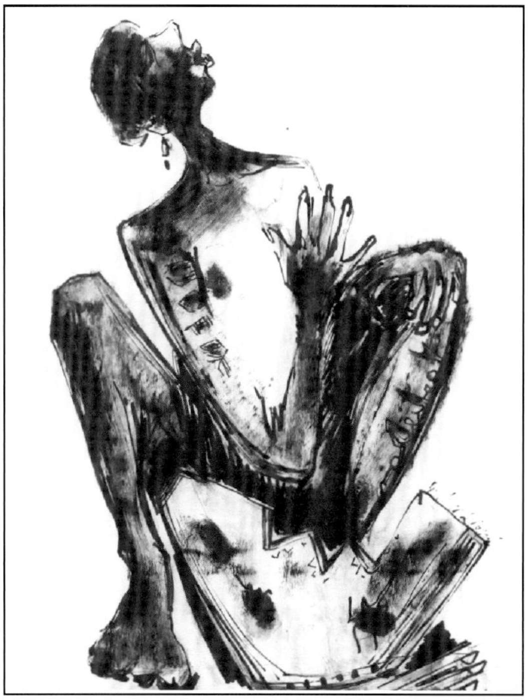

Rainmaker. Felt pen & watercolour. 1966, Adelaide. 76.0 x 61.0 cm. Private collection, Adelaide. Photograph: Graeme Hastwell.

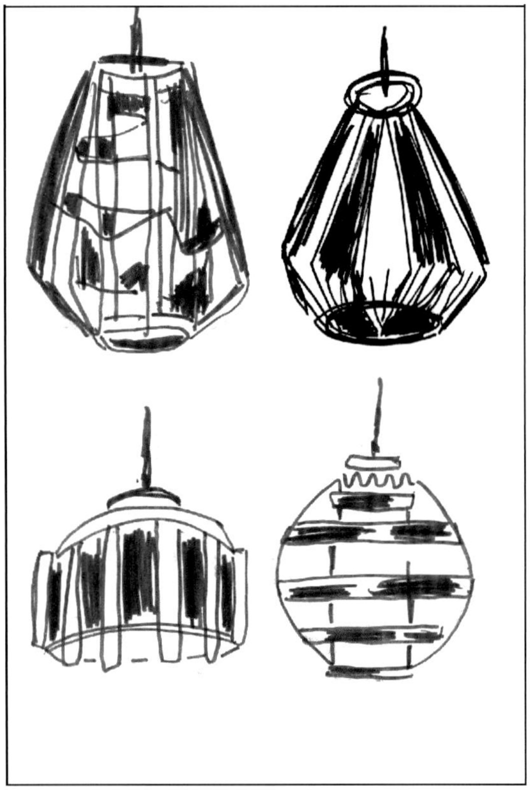

Sketches for copper lamps designs. Felt pen on paper. ca.1967, Adelaide. 29.3 x 21.0 cm. Dutkiewicz Archive.

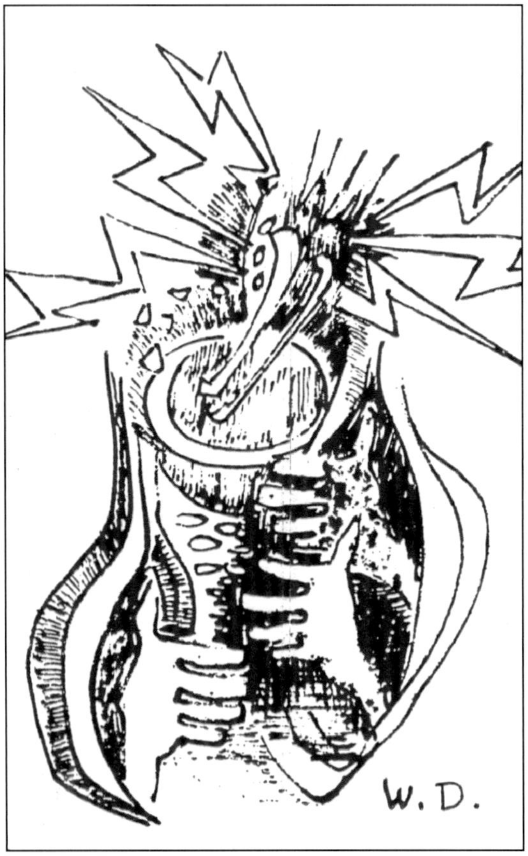

Catalogue design. *Duda* (Polish bagpipes). Printed pen & ink drawing. 1966, Adelaide. Dutkiewicz Archive.

This statement shows his intensity and his risk-taking, and perhaps prophetically anticipated his future, when he lost that earthly support. He also wrote: "Art is ... a spiritual act – a contemplation committing body and spirit together ... man expressing himself at his highest but most fragile level where matter and the unknown unite" and where "the striving of substance and the concentration of spirit" is inseparable.[7]

To Wlad, Art was not just important, it was essential. It was where humanity recorded its experience and dreams, and pushed itself to its imaginative limits. It was the twin sister of Science and Philosophy, a site of documentation of the life of the free mind. His art was not about dogma, but its rhetoric was of humanitarianism and the celebration of people and life. He was not a cynic and his art was not about being superficial and coolly ironic: it was poetic, dramatic and lyrical, and it often harnessed a gentle, satirical humour. With such a philosophy, Wlad was not a man for the twenty-first century: he did not possess a television and I doubt if he would have recognized a computer. He was a committed bohemian, a profoundly individual and radical person. I believe Wlad revelled in his freedom, above all else: nothing else mattered but making art.

He treasured living in Australia where he could be himself. He rejected the options of America and Europe, and Stalinist and Communist Poland were not for him, even though, as a patriot, he pined for his homeland. He was a proud Pole, a refugee and enemy of the KGB, and could never completely feel at home in his new country, always torn in heart and mind between two ideologies and cultures. He was also a "character," someone who stood out in the crowd and was regarded with some suspicion by the conservative, Anglophile burgers of the city-state.

My mother deserves considerable credit for recognizing his quality and helping him. She did everything she could and much more than any reasonable human being would do. Wlad may have had his disappointments, especially in terms of the reception of his art outside of Adelaide, where he was a star, but with her help he achieved remarkable things. And before he became too twisted with alcohol and disappointments he was grateful to Joan: "An artist's life is usually not easy. My wife works hard. She understands my joys and sorrows. Painting can be selfish and possessive, and fortunate is the artist who has a tolerant wife. I am lucky ..." [8]

It is a pity that the rest of Australia has not appreciated my father's art as much as many people have in Adelaide, until recent decades. I know he was grateful for the friendships and encouragement he received here from many of his colleagues and patrons. There were barriers in the Anglocentric culture of the southern capital, but they were not as great as he found in the eastern states' cities.

In the end I believe he was happy to live in a place where he had made a contribution and where he had been, to some extent at least, appreciated. I believe that is why he never left, even though he slipped into relative obscurity as the fashions in the art world shifted towards Pop, Hard-Edge, Conceptualism, Minimalism and Political art. Of course, all of these artistic ideologies were anathema and destructive to him, as they promoted an oppositional view to the one he cherished, of generosity of imagination and human spirit and commitment to individuality and creativity.

[7] WEA lecture, "Visiting the Art Galleries" series, ca.1974.

[8] W. Dutkiewicz, Interview in the *Advertiser*, 12 December 1959, 17.

When I contacted Wlad's greatest collector, who resides in Perth, in the week before he died, she said to tell him that his art brought great joy to her and her husband's life and to the life of their children. The same is true for many of us here in Adelaide, and to a lesser extent on the east coast, where there are numerous works in private collections.

Wlad was extremely difficult to bear in the 1970s and 1980s, when I struck out to pursue my own interests in life and to find my way as a painter too, but in later years, especially after receiving treatment for alcoholism in 1988-89, he was productive and approachable again.

From that time, I prepared four major retrospective exhibitions for him in various venues in Adelaide. Finally, when my own health deserted me in the late 1990s, around the time of the last of these surveys, our contact diminished until he resembled a colourful old kite on a vast string, drifting further and further into the sky. Eventually, I could no longer gather the string, and he drifted away from me. However, my second sister, Anna, gently kept him within tether until the end.

Wlad created a remarkable life for his children, although occasionally excellent in its poverty, to paraphrase the great Irish comic novelist, Flann O'Brien, in his novel *The Poor Mouth.* In the last few decades it became somewhat nightmarish as the psychic negativity, physical vicissitudes of old age, and ghosts of the past haunted him.

In the end, and he was on his own for the last decade, it was truly as if he was living out a role from Maxim Gorky's *The Lower Depths*, which he produced as a fringe production for the Adelaide Festival in 1960. That play described a lifestyle completely incomprehensible to middle class and well-to-do Australians. Despite the tribulations, his children, friends and admirers love him for the good times, the wonderful memories and for what he did, and for his artistic legacy, which will continue to inspire those who know it. He left a better world behind him. He did many great things in a world in which it is difficult to achieve just one.

I thank him for his lack of affectations and the gamut of emotions offered by his wonderful, imaginative life. Through this book, and in revealing what I discovered about his life over the last twenty years and my selection of paintings, sculptures and graphics, I hope others will come to appreciate his contribution.

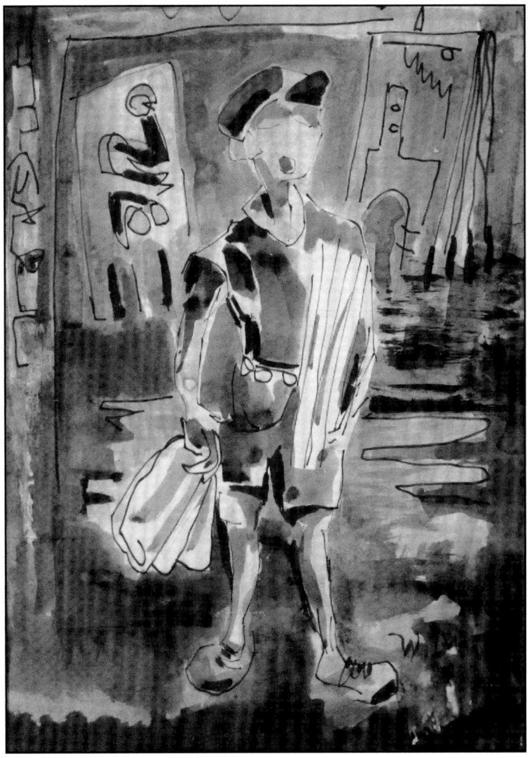

Newsboy. Felt pen, coloured inks on paper. 1966, Adelaide. 65.0 x 46.0 cm. Private collection. Photograph: Graeme Hastwell.

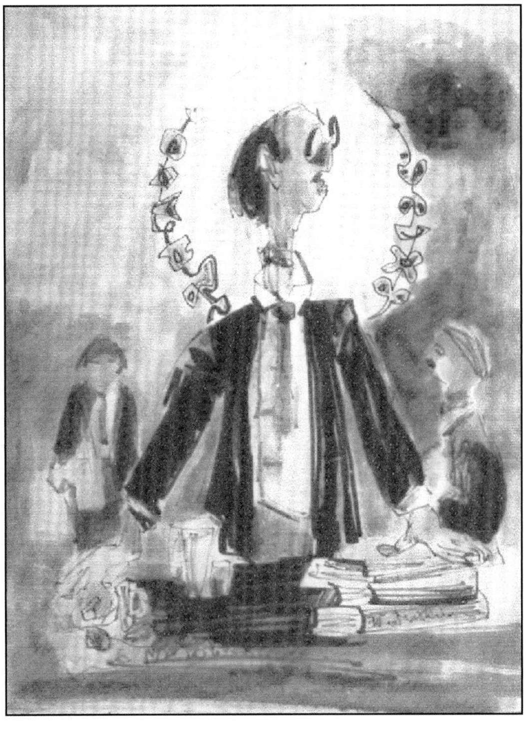

Politician. Felt pen, coloured inks on paper. ca.1970, Adelaide. 69.0 x 55.0 cm. Estate of the artist. Photograph: Graeme Hastwell.

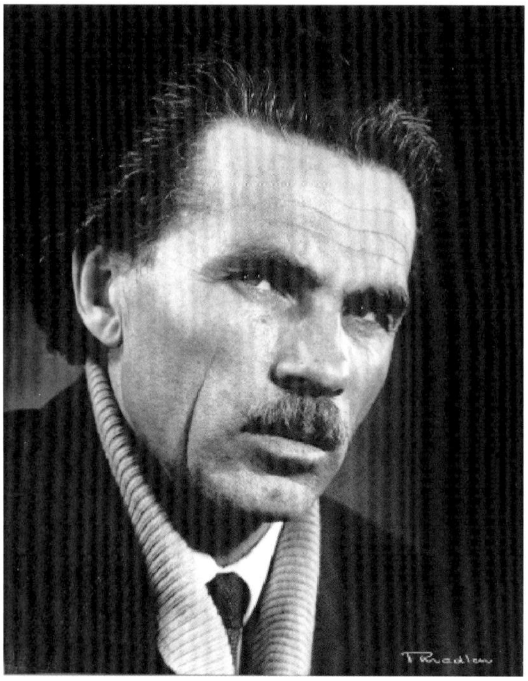

Peter Medlen. *Wladyslaw Dutkiewicz*. Black and white photographic print. 1962, Adelaide. 50.0 x 40.0 cm. Estate of the artist.

Wladyslaw Dutkiewicz

Excerpt from an Interview with Hazel de Berg for the National Library of Australia, 10th August 1962

The arts in Europe have a potential influence on every child and every young artist there. Of course the galleries and the museums give you a terrific impact, you see that everything has already been done, you see everything that famous people have achieved, and that you are probably able to copy, probably you are able to achieve the technical level, you can learn that, but then you always have to ask the question: what about me?

I already had achieved something in my drawing, in my painting, in my colour, but then I read a book by Vassily Kandinsky called "The Spiritual Harmony", which brought me something that has affected me today: the ideas of new forms, a new art, and it says in there clearly that something that has been done should not be repeated.

I started to study this deeply and I think I achieved something. What I got is that art cannot be separated from philosophy, so after studying that a little bit and adopting simple thinking or clear thinking, and with time to grasp what our big fathers like Aristotle and Plato have left for us, I came to the conclusion that Kandinsky is right, that his idea is not yet accomplished but it can be done, we can combine the arts with philosophy.

If, for instance, we say that philosophy has the elements of hypothesis, thesis, antithesis, there is still something lacking there: synthesis. One could ask how I try in practice to apply these philosophical elements and make them workable in a picture.

For me, hypothesis is the work of a child: the child assumes, the child tries; she has no ideas probably already established, but she tries. Thesis, it is art of the past, it is classical example; everything that is done from the Greek time up to the 18th and 19th centuries has thesis, it possesses all ... the qualifications of art. Antithesis was born with the impressionists. They drew the conclusion that thesis was classically well established, and it must be broken; there is still something else that the human being has to say, has to do. But now synthesis: even though the abstract art and all the "ism" art forms have been born, the synthesis of the abstraction has not been found, and this synthesis I am looking for.

I am doing just a simple thing. For me the imaginary starting points are very essential. The starting point, I mean, can be here – my bus or this cigarette, as the first one – the second can be possibly Port Adelaide or even Darwin; and if I join these two points in a first line, a straight one, my imagination is directed strongly towards each one; then the second line, it will be a curve, it will be probably, for example, to fly by the aeroplane, and if I combine these two lines with my starting points, the sphere in between starts to design for me a picture, in essence.

And if I still find more points and dislodge them, I have more and more that is coming as an image.

Therefore today, in this time when man is moving into space ... an artist is starting to look somewhere else and he cannot find a new form if he doesn't accept this synthesis. He would have difficulty in any country to be a painter, a painter of today.

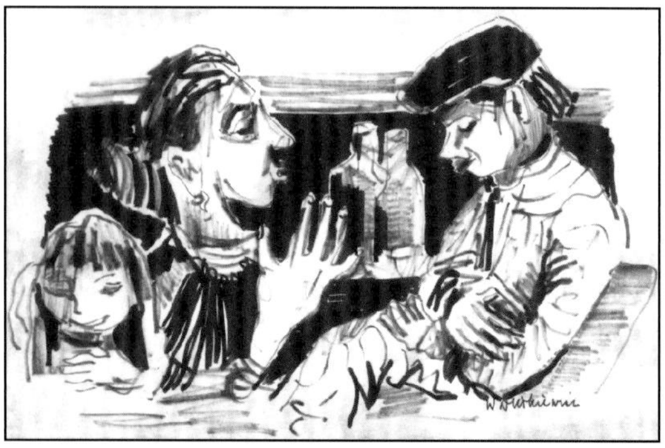

Argument. Felt pen on paper. ca.1968, Adelaide. approx. 39.0 x 50.0 cm. Private collection, Adelaide. Photograph: Graeme Hastwell.

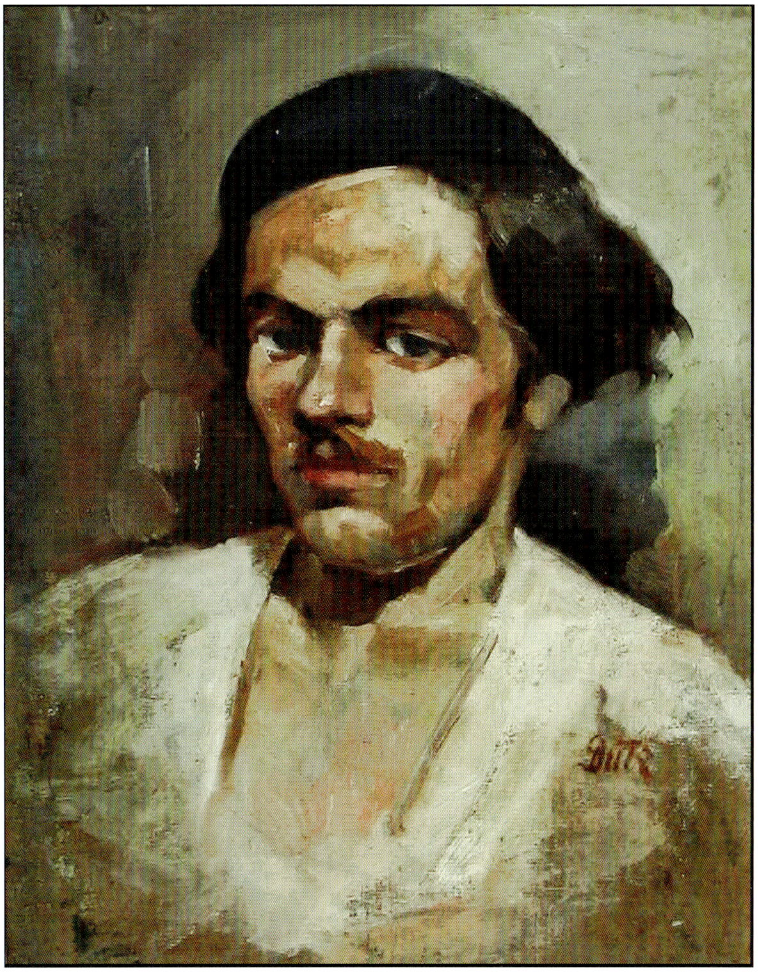

Self portrait. Oil on canvas on composition board. 1945, Hohenfels, Germany.
45.0 x 35.0 cm. Estate of the artist. Photograph: Graeme Hastwell.

Germany Series, 1945-49

Paintings from the Major Series

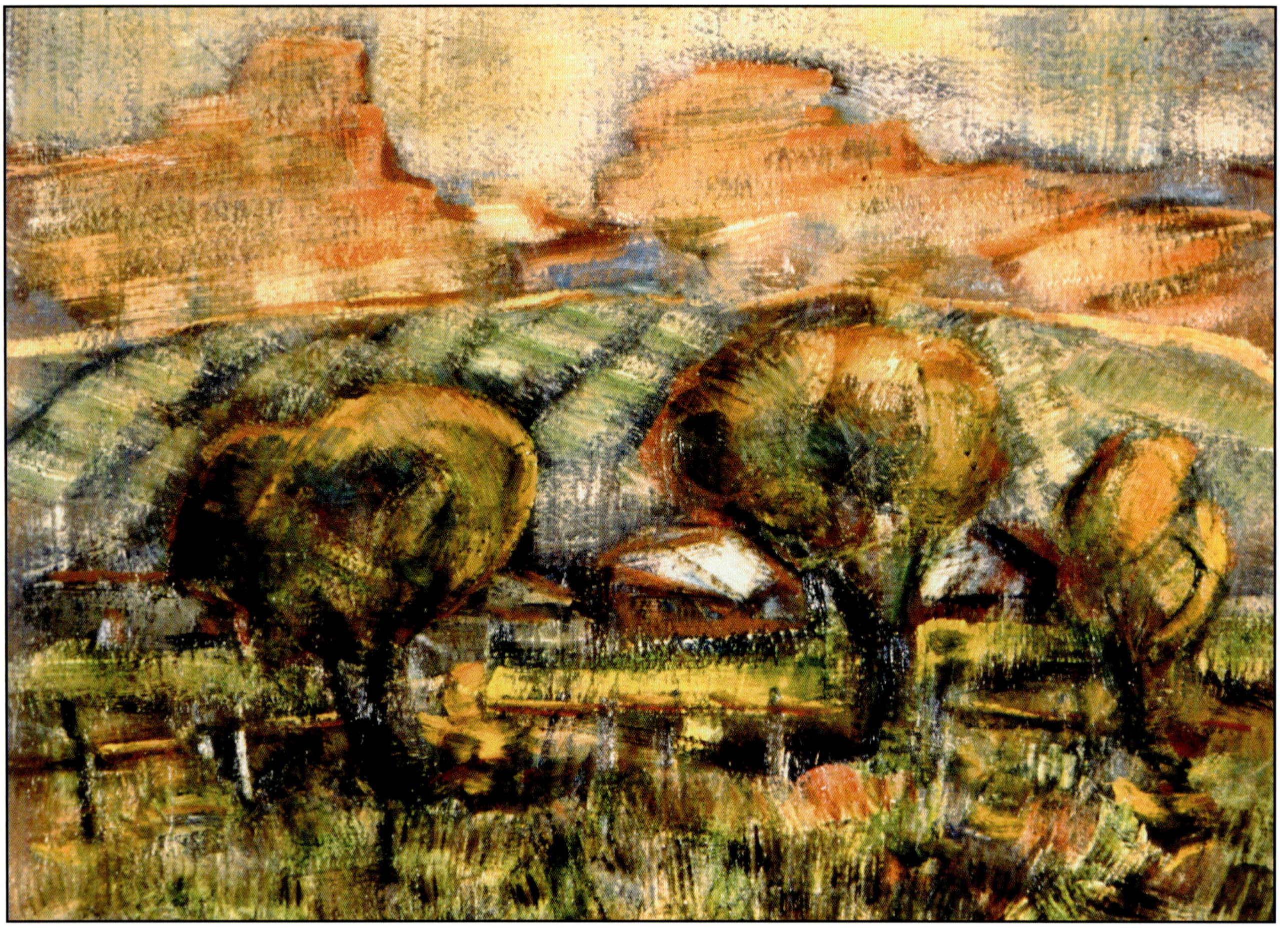

Daybreak. Oil on paperboard. 1950, Adelaide. 52.0 x 72.0 cm. Estate of the artist.
Photograph: Stephanie Schrapel.

A rhythmic painting in a style closer to the Australian Post-Impressionists, specifically Grace Cossington-Smith. Tightly controlled in tone and texture, it evokes the golden colours of the wheat-belt set seemingly incongruously under the shadow of distant, ancient rock forms. The use of dry brush coveys the semi-arid atmosphere, and the frosting of lighter colours over the background tones serves dual purposes: to depict the cast of light and the texture of dry grasses and crops.

Early Australian Landscape Series, 1950

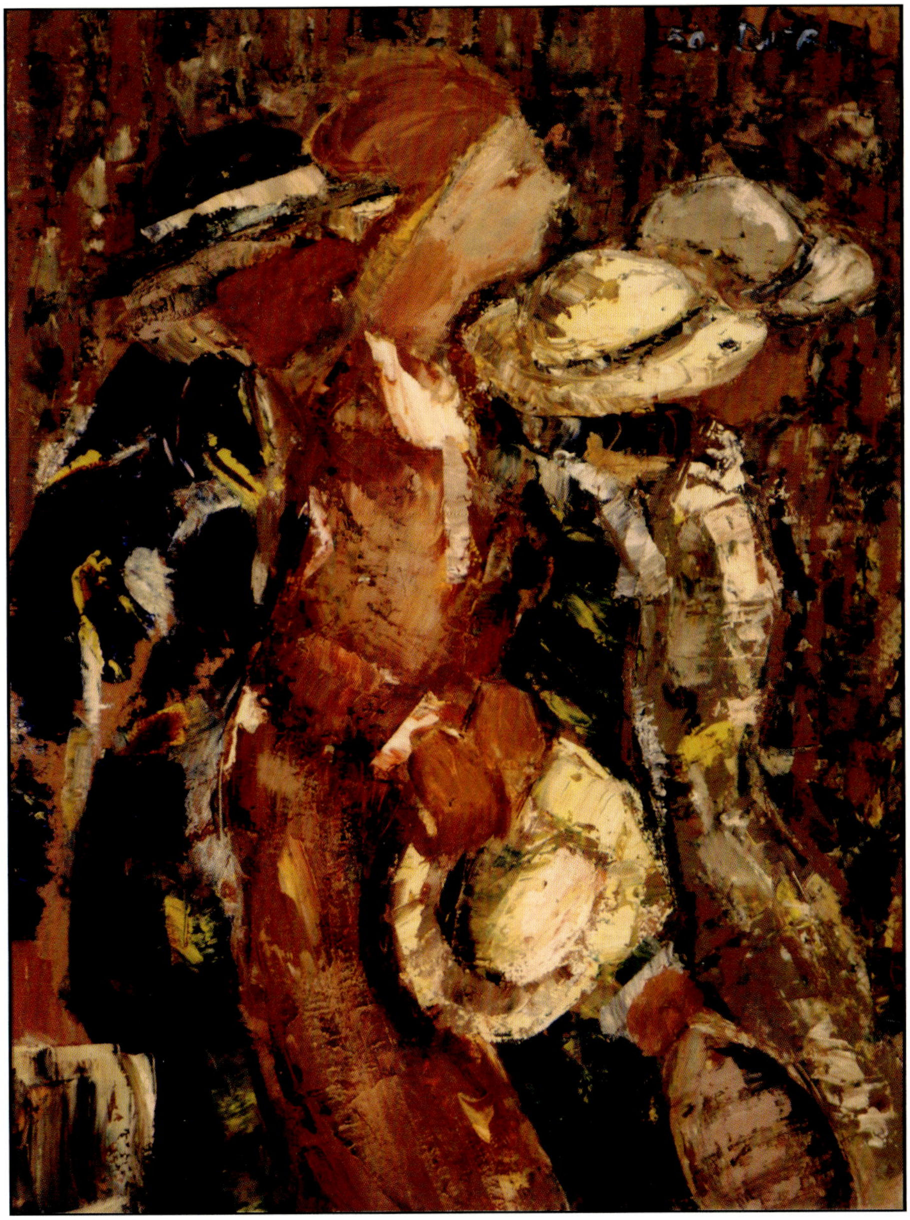

Exam fever. Oil on balsa wood. 1950, Adelaide. 59.5 x 45.5 cm.
Private collection, Adelaide. Photograph: Graeme Hastwell.

A lively and somewhat conventional painting, referring to late 19th century Impressionism, showing four teenage girls in uniform dashing for an examination. The movement in the painting is largely implied, and a sense of urgency, apprehension and concentration is locked into the facial expression of the red-haired girl in the central foreground.

Schoolgirls Series, 1950

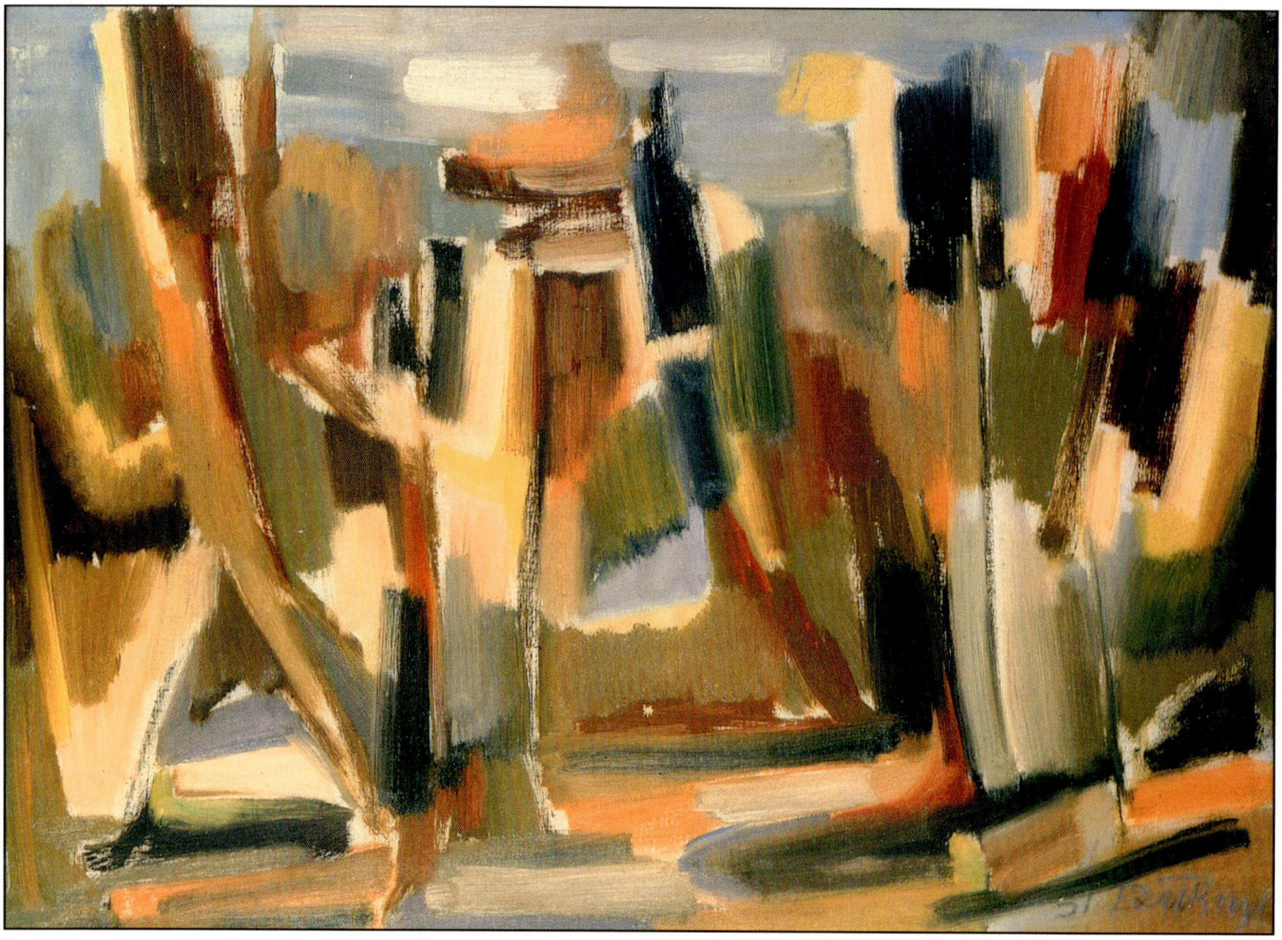

Bush. Oil on canvas. 1951, Adelaide. 62.2 x 85.1 cm. Private collection, Brisbane. Photograph: Graeme Hastwell.

Here Wlad honed his palette to earth tones of browns, ochres and the grey-greens of eucalypt and scrub, in a freed-up, yet organized arrangement of unrestrained, large brushstrokes. The landscape is reduced to its simplest elements: tonal colour, verticality and horizontality, and dryness. This approach was modelled on a watercolour he had painted at Murnau (p. 54) in 1945, when visiting the studio of Gabrielle Münter and viewing Wassily Kandinsky's work of his Blaue Reiter period, in that he had broken away from the literal and sought the essence of what he was painting. It was shown in his first major exhibition in 1951: it was a radical departure from the pedantic realism in landscape painting to which South Australian audiences were so accustomed at that time, in the form of the Hans Heysen School.

First Abstracted Landscape Series, 1951

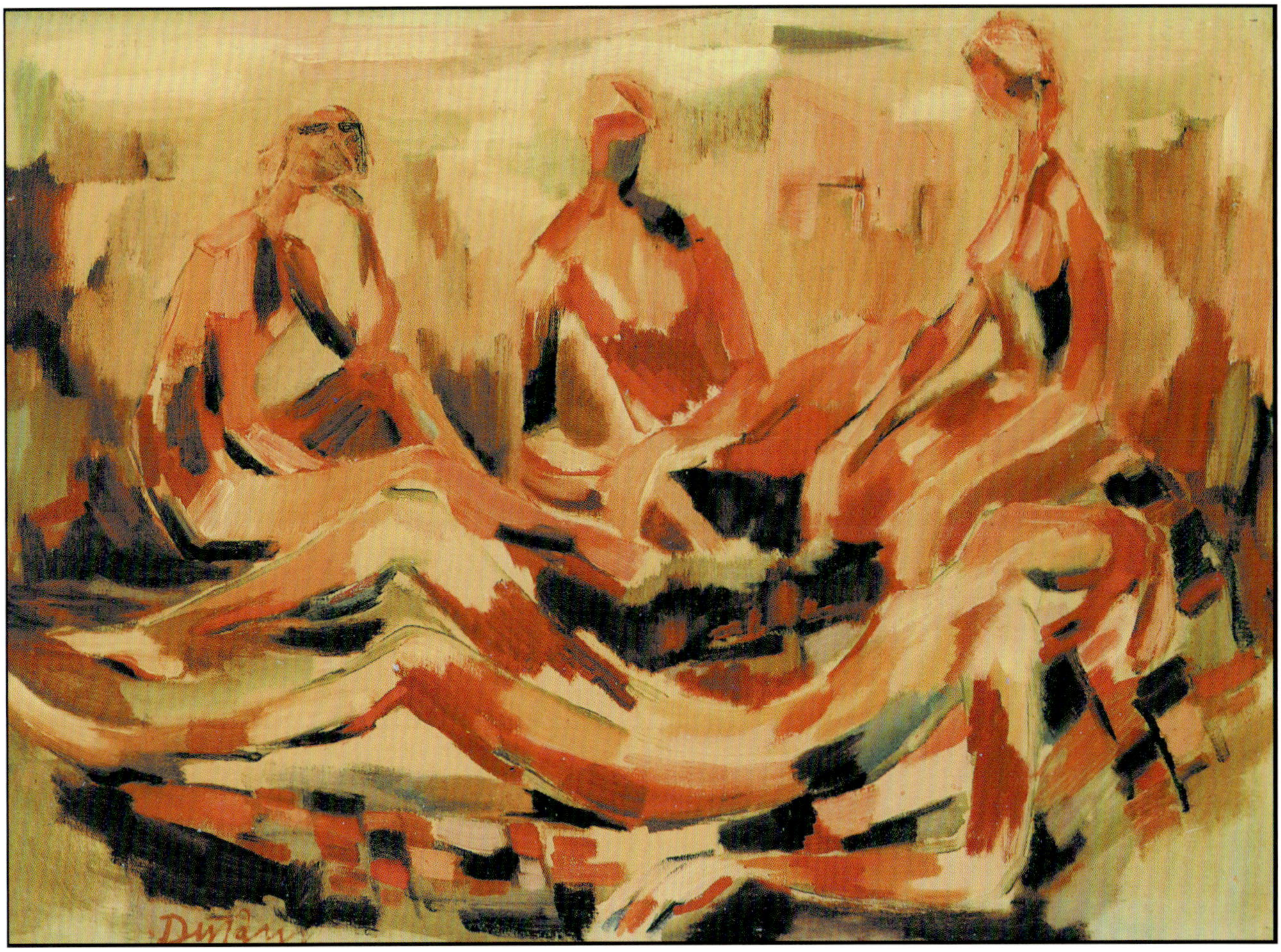

Bathers. Oil on canvas. ca.1952, Adelaide. 64.8 x 90.2 cm. Private collection, Adelaide. Photograph: Graeme Hastwell.

A sophisticated fusion of Expressionism and Abstraction but in figurative mode, at the same time referring to Cézanne's paintings on the same theme, yet tonally hotter: an arid version, if you like, limited to the colours of sand, sun and tanned skin.

First Abstracted Figurative Series, 1952-54

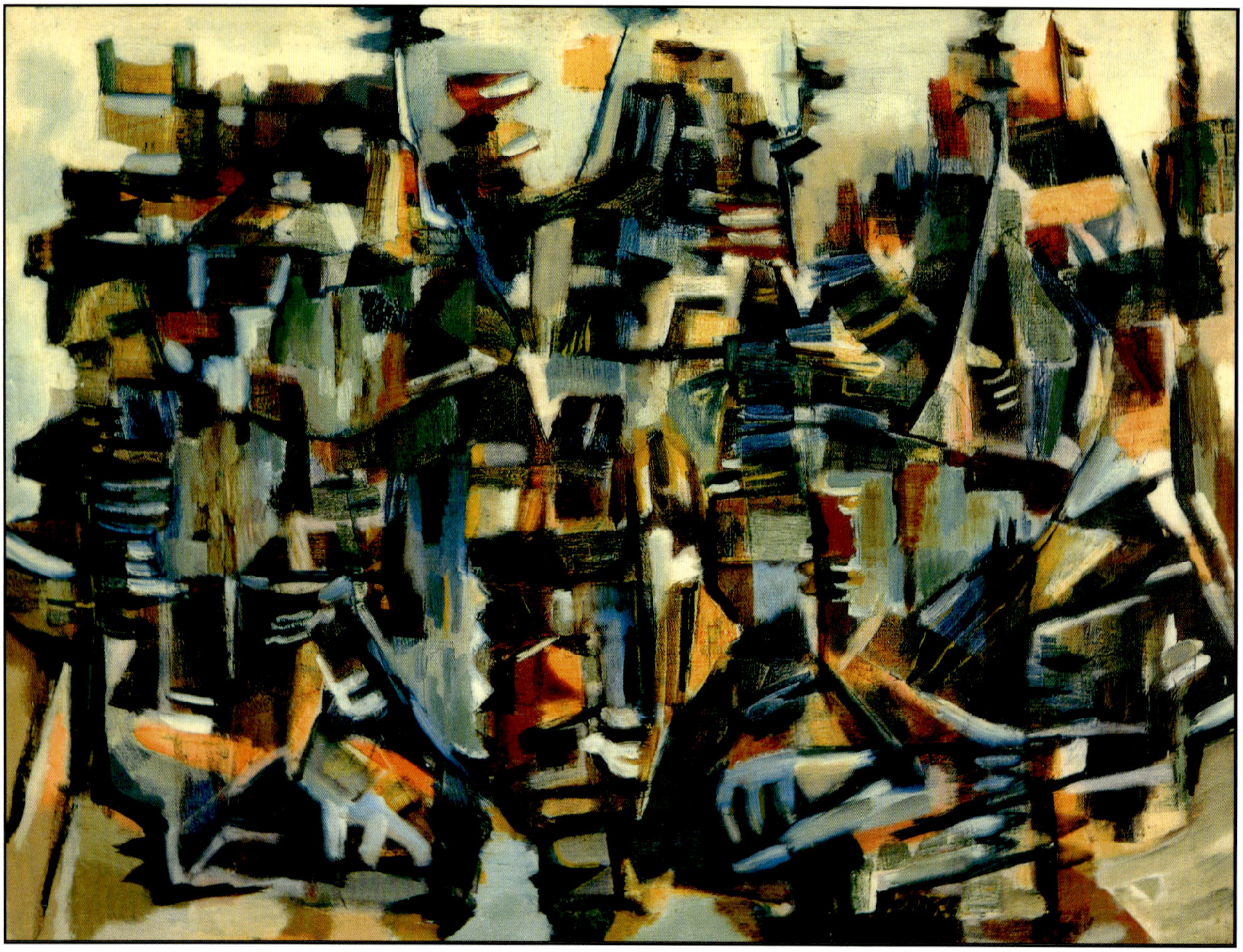

Orient. Oil on canvas. 1955, Adelaide. 79.0 x 103.0 cm. Private collection, Adelaide.
Photograph: Graeme Hastwell.

Painted with spontaneity but nevertheless a highly refined tonal composition, this picture is one of several with an architectural orientation painted at that time. It won the Contemporary Art Society of South Australia's Cornell Prize in 1955.

Architectural Series, 1954-55

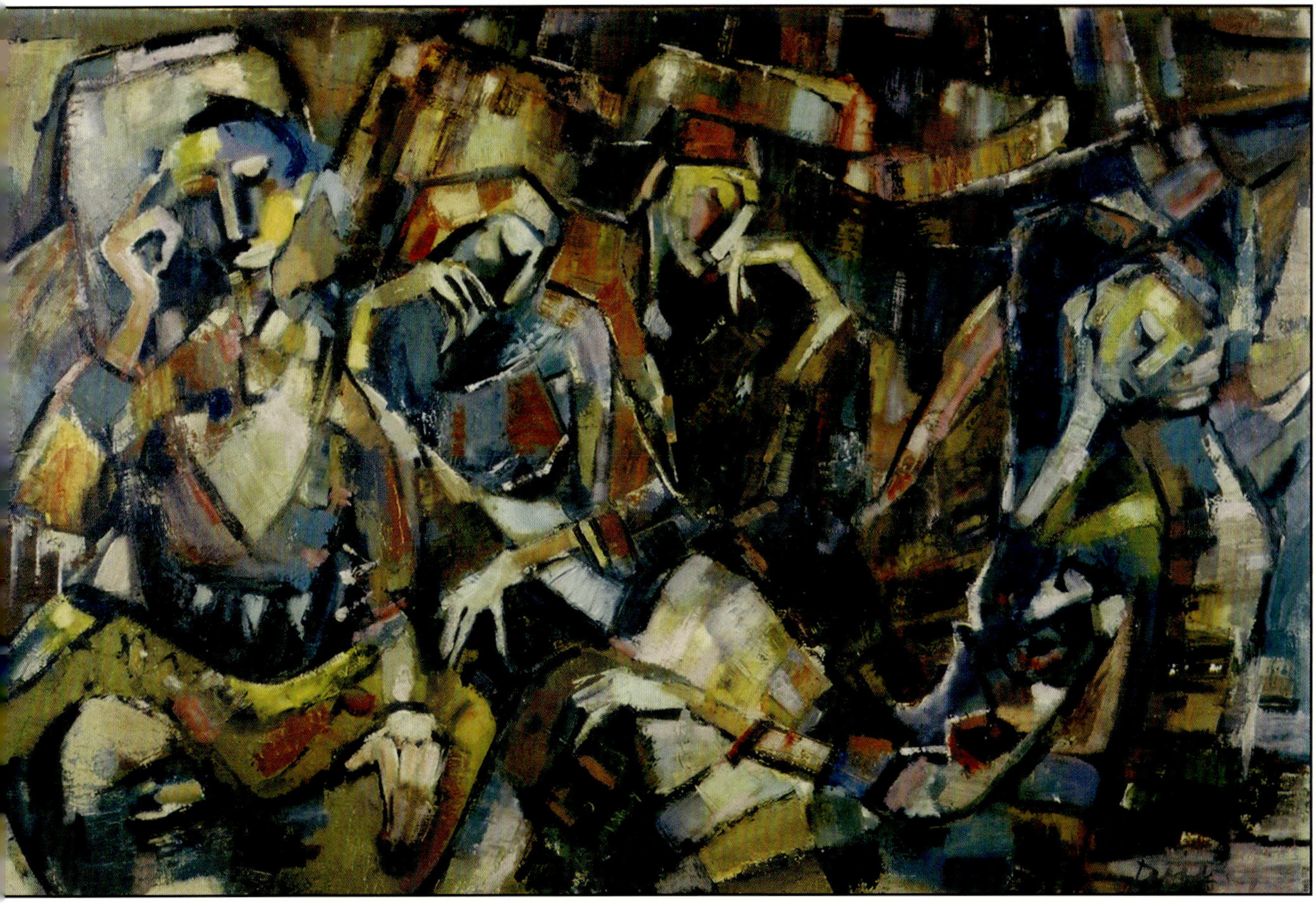

Travellers. Oil on composition board. 1956, Adelaide. 91.5 x 137.0 cm. Estate of the artist.
Photograph: Graeme Hastwell.

In this painting Wlad operates in a Romanesque-inspired mode. He has taken care to define all the forms and to render the hands with particular definition. It is more aesthetically integrated, using a combination of brushes and palette knives, and less loosely expressionistic than an earlier work, *Madonna and child*, and his painting selected as a finalist in the Blake Prize of the same year, *Healing of the Sick*. He returned to this theme in the mid 1960s to complete a suite of felt pen and coloured ink drawings based on the Apostles, the Madonna and the Angels.

Religious Series, 1954-56

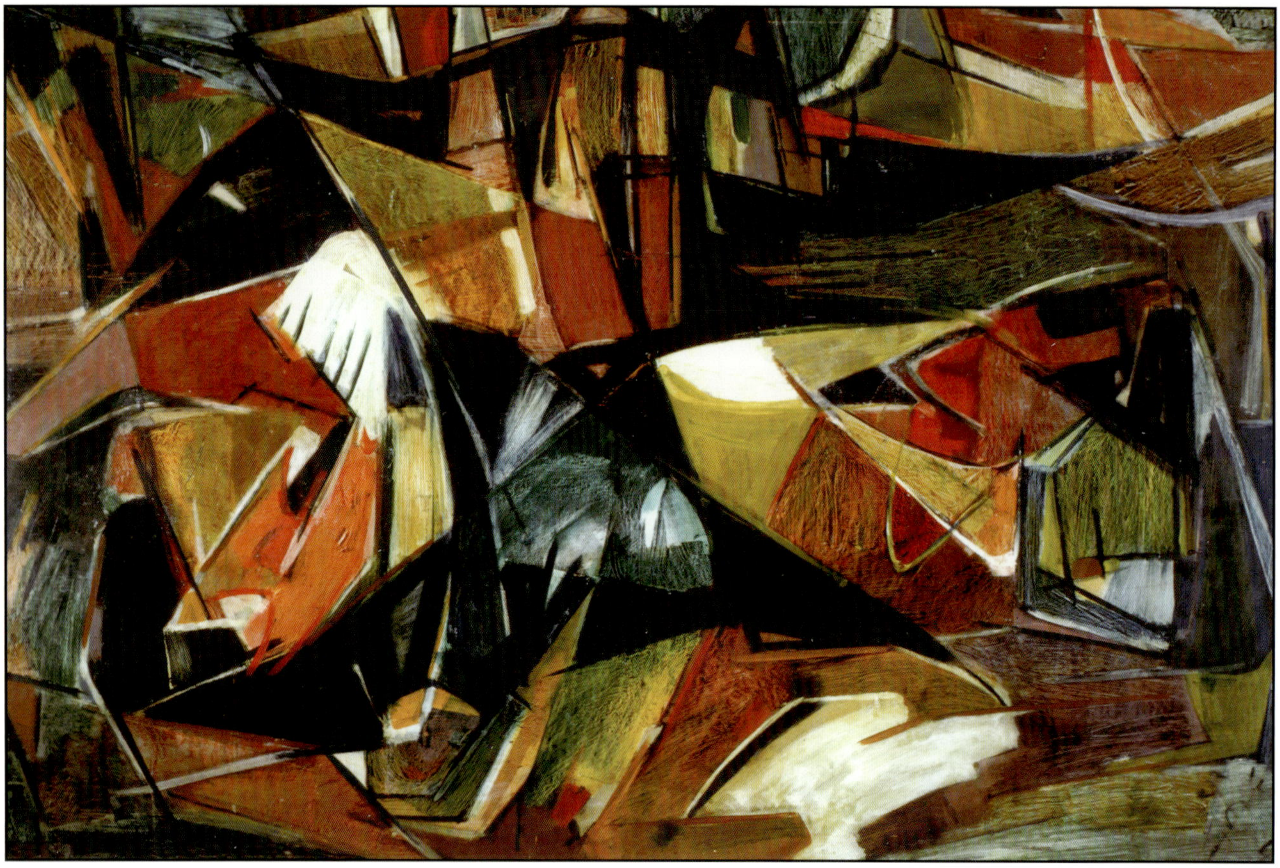

For Stravinsky. Oil on composition board. 1954, Adelaide. 132.0 x 208.0 cm. Estate of the artist.
Photograph: Graeme Hastwell.

I regard this as Wlad's first major work, as it brings together in one canvas all the possibilities he had discovered in the abstract into a symphonic whole, using his "cosmic theories of light and line". Note the combination of brush and scraper work, and the use of *sgraffito* (scratching back or otherwise revealing deeper layers) and unusual textures applied to otherwise more conventional, albeit soft-geometrical, Constructivist ideas of interpenetrating planes of colour.

Another signal as to its importance is the shift in signature, from the "Dutkie" he first used to the initialled format seen on lower right, which was subsequently simplified to side-be-side initials (in a few cases inverted). Although the previous signature was used occasionally after, it was phased out by about 1956, with one or two exceptions and variations. Later, in the early 1970s, he began signing his initials with felt pen, and a number of earlier unsigned paintings were thus signed from that time onward.

Musical Abstracts Series, 1954-56

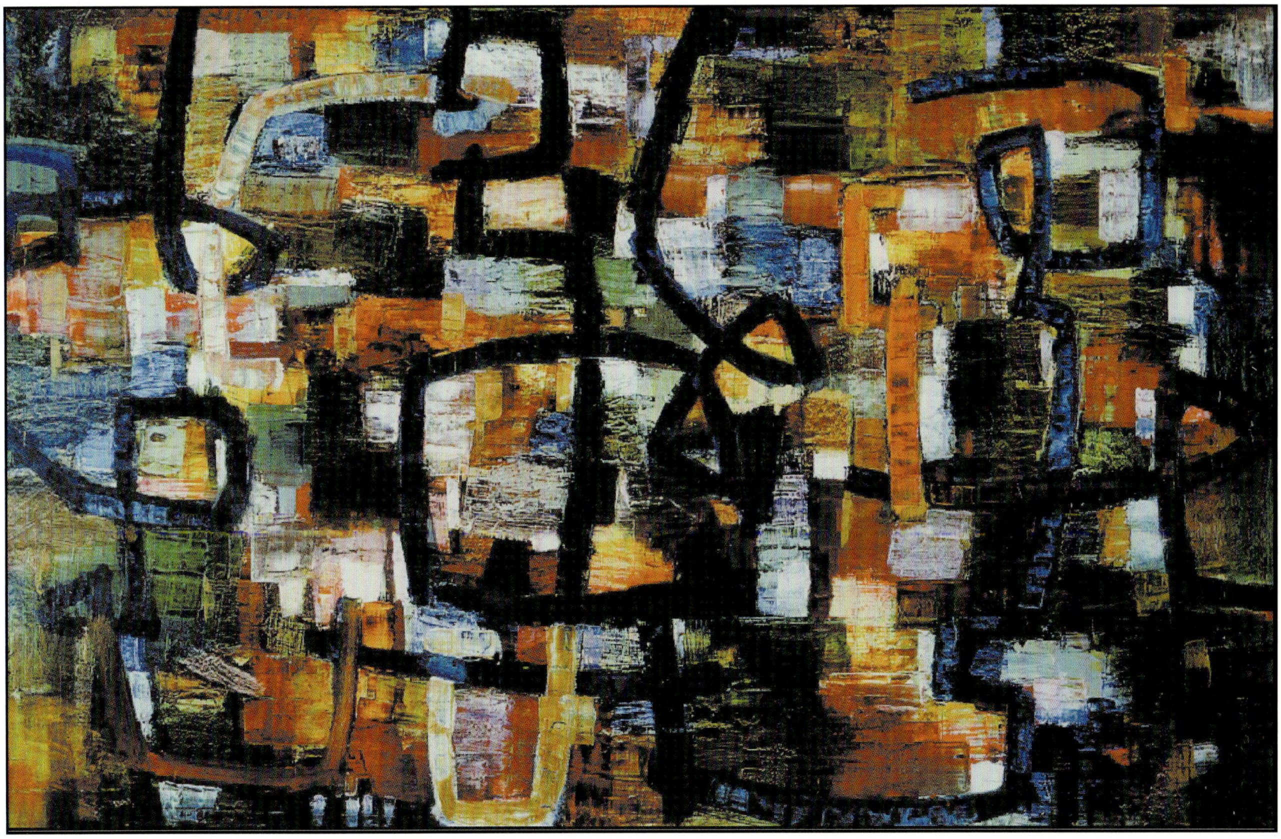

City at night. Oil on composition board. ca.1956, Adelaide. 91.5 x 137.0 cm. Estate of the artist. Photograph: Graeme Hastwell.

Here the artist selects organic colours from the Australian environment and, using a variety of scrapers and knives, fuses to this palette the styles of late Mondrian and de Staël. There are obvious similarities with *Calligraphy* (AGSA), *Shapes in Space* (see *The Encyclopedia of Australian Art*, 1st ed.) and his murals of the preceding years. The signature top left is in the old style. He completed several works that gravitated more closely to de Staël's style in the early 1960s, clearly more tachiste in orientation than much of his work.

Organic Constructivism Series, 1952-56

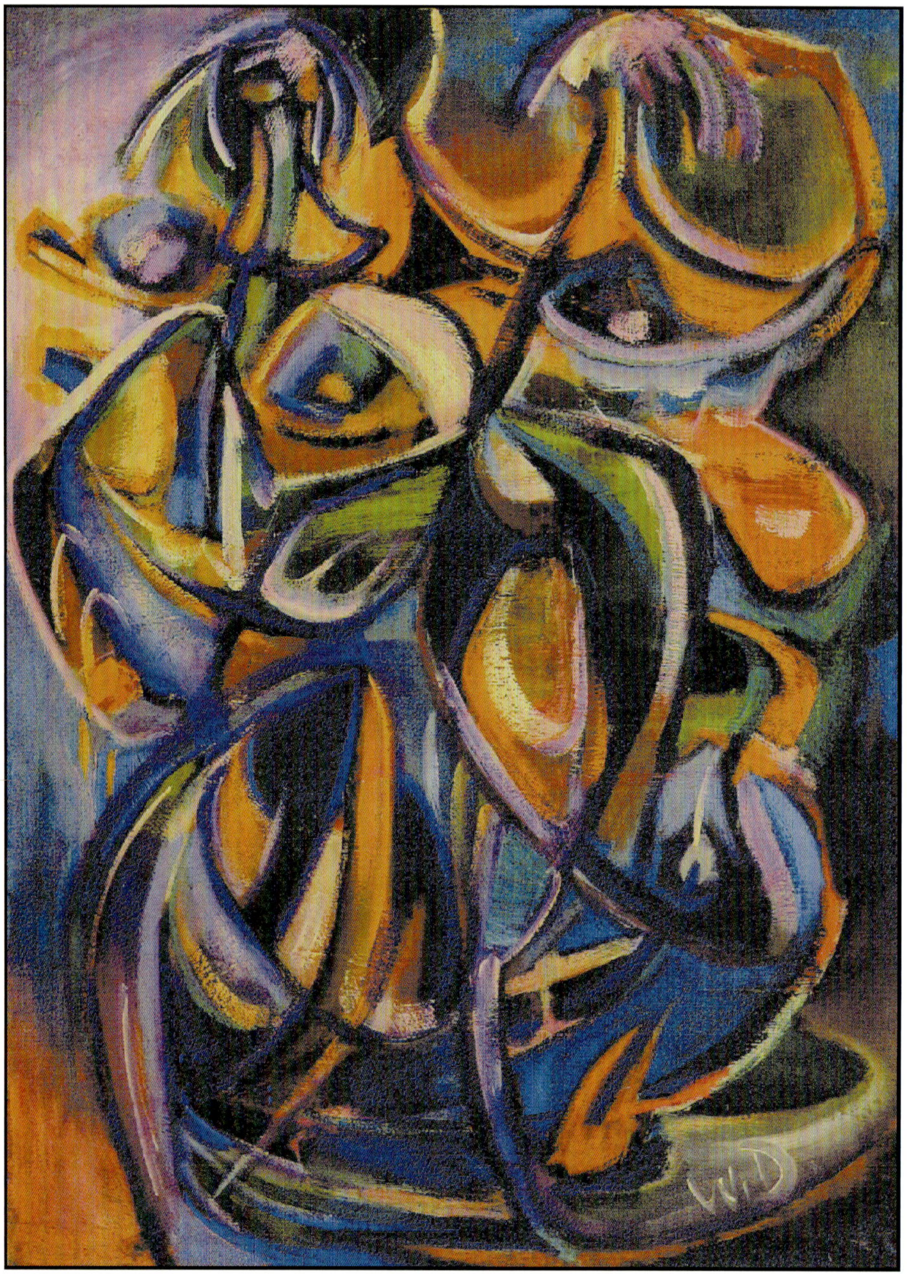

Dancing Figures/Pair. Oil on canvas. 1956, Adelaide. 86.0 x 62.0 cm. Private collection, Adelaide. Photograph: Graeme Hastwell.

These abstracted figures refer to his wire and gauze sculpture series from the 6th Architectural Convention Exhibition, Botanic Park, Adelaide, June 1956. This one was also known as *Adam & Eve*, since the original sculptural pieces were located in a garden setting in the open. The figure grouping was recycled later in the principal painting in the Hunters series (p. 35).

Architectural Convention & Related Figurative Series, 1956

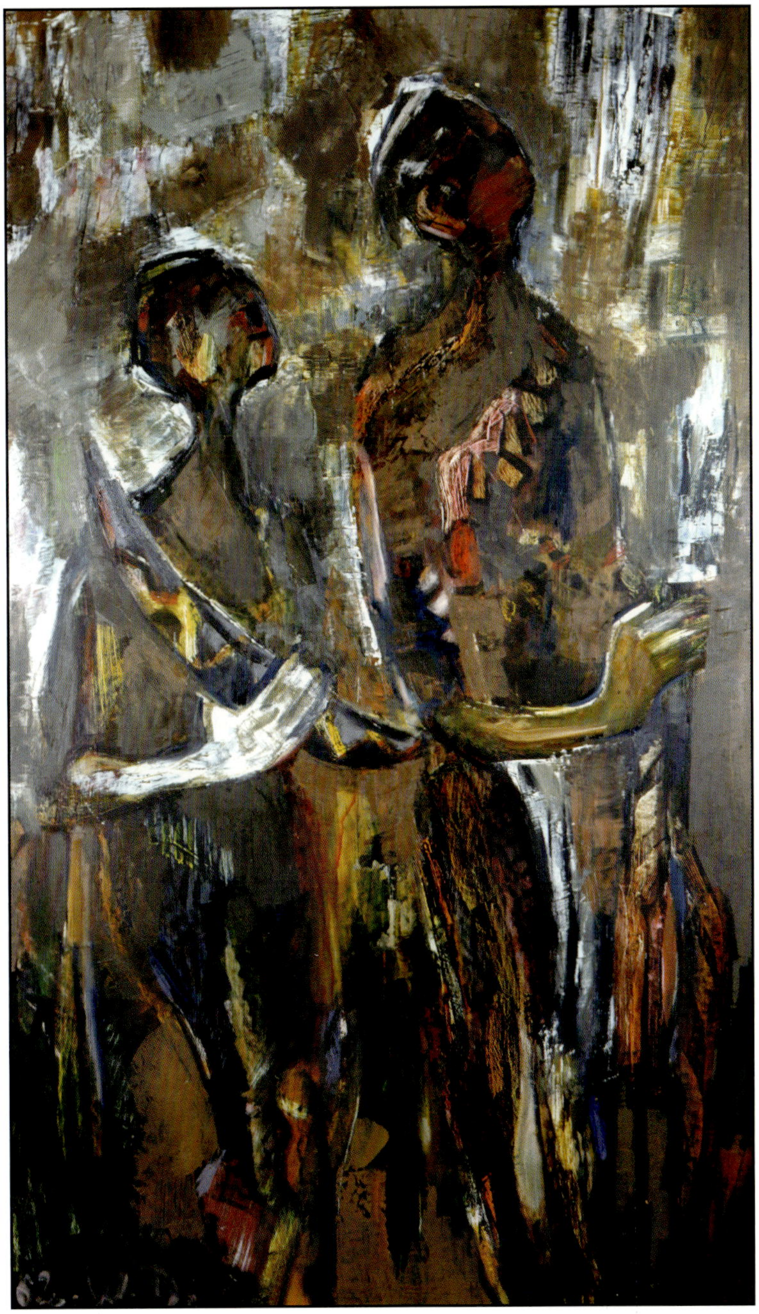

Hunters [I]. Oil on composition board. 1962, Adelaide. 136.0 x 81.5 cm. Private collection, Adelaide. Photograph: Graeme Hastwell.

Wlad's subject here is two Aboriginal males, with boomerang and woomera, standing together like a termite mound in the desert while stalking a kangaroo or emu. A second large painting in this series shows a similar Aboriginal group gathered near a wurlie. A more abstract and visually dynamic work from this series, depicting the nocturnal action of a corroboree, now resides in Glasgow.

Hunters Series, 1962

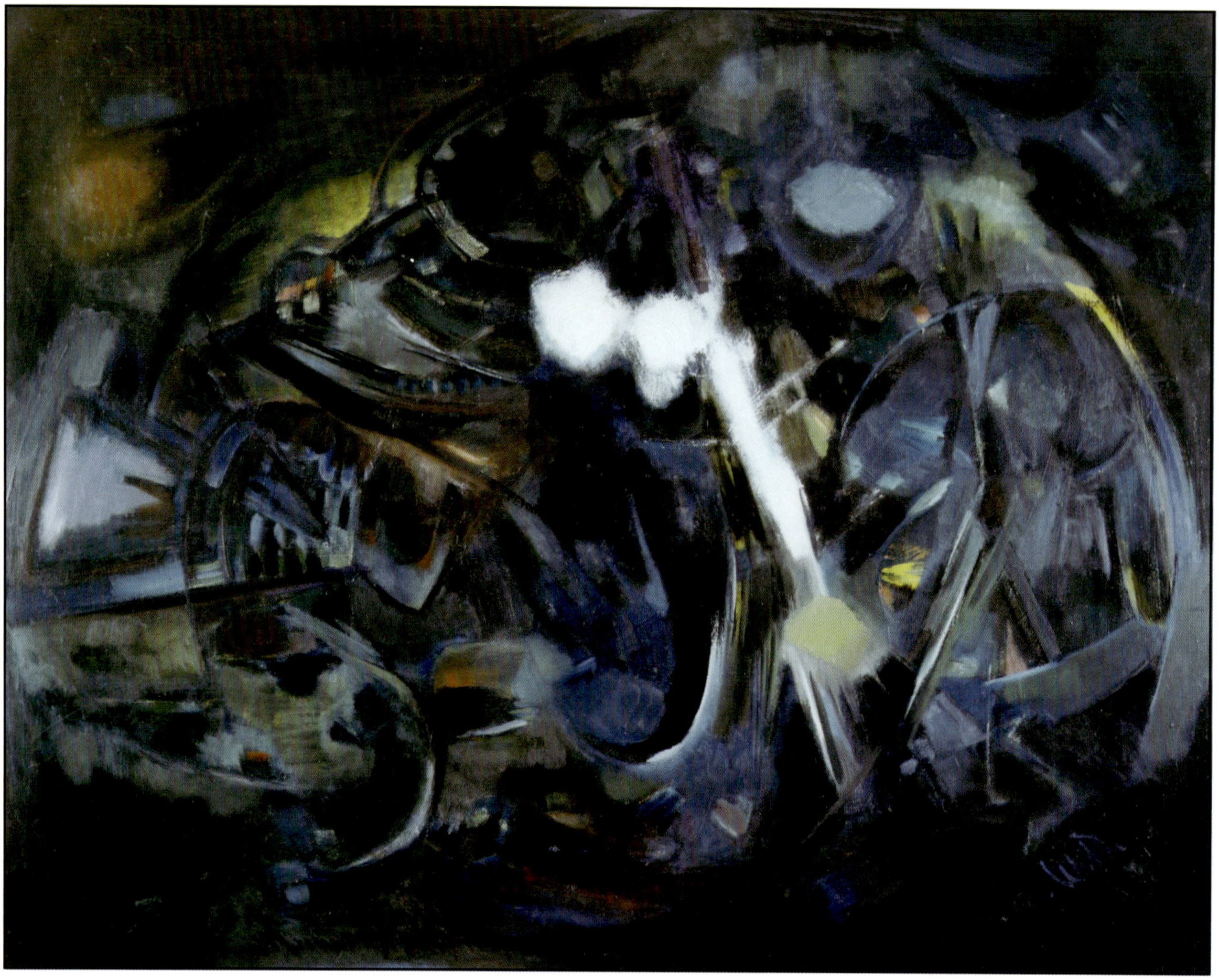

In Orbit. Oil on composition board. 1960, Adelaide. 104.0 x 134.5 cm. Estate of the artist. Photograph: Graeme Hastwell.

An excursion into space and blackness, which the artist said does not exist. Note the large circular form, presumably the earth, behind which there is a hint of sun. His inspiration came with the launch of the first "animalled" flight satellite, *Sputnik V*, on 20th August 1960. Wlad envisioned the voyage in the darkness of deep space as a metaphor for his own recovery from his motorcycle accident in June 1956, and projected his imagination into that place, showing us both the space-capsule and it travelling at high speed as a flash of light across the sky. In terms of art history interesting comparisons with this image exist in some of the paintings of the Chilean-born surrealist Matta. He painted a very similar work concerning the Snowy Mountains Irrigation Scheme at the same time as well as pictures about nuclear reactors, bulldozers and modern, if not futuristic, architecture.

Modern Technology Series, ca.1960

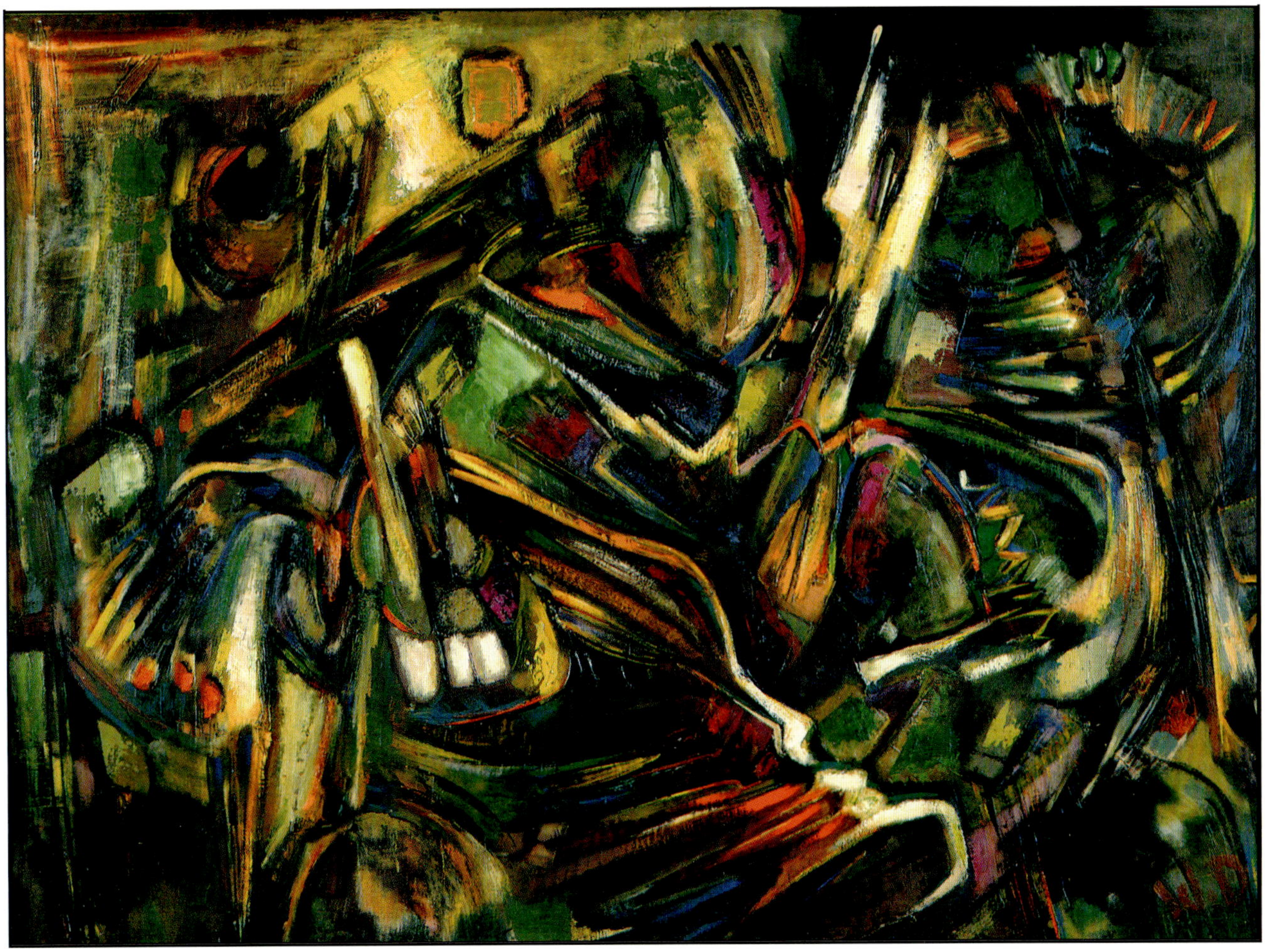

Vibrato. Oil on composition board. 1962, Adelaide. 84.0 x 115.5 cm. Estate of the artist. Photograph: Graeme Hastwell.

An evocation of nature and the vibration of the spirit. The space is an organic world alive with an electrical energy, with a mysterious light permeating deeply the layered dimensions, as if in the middle of dank, dark forest, caught in an imaginary cobweb disturbed by the beating wing and shrieking call of a native bird. Again, the palette impinges on black, without ever using it: there are deep umbers, greens and shadowy blues, energised by strategically placed flashes of white and bright colour. This is one of Wlad's most exciting, essential and individuated works: it resembles in mood and substance, if anything in terms of art history, some of the fantastic, convoluted landscapes of Max Ernst.

ORGANIC ABSTRACTS SERIES, EARLY 1960S

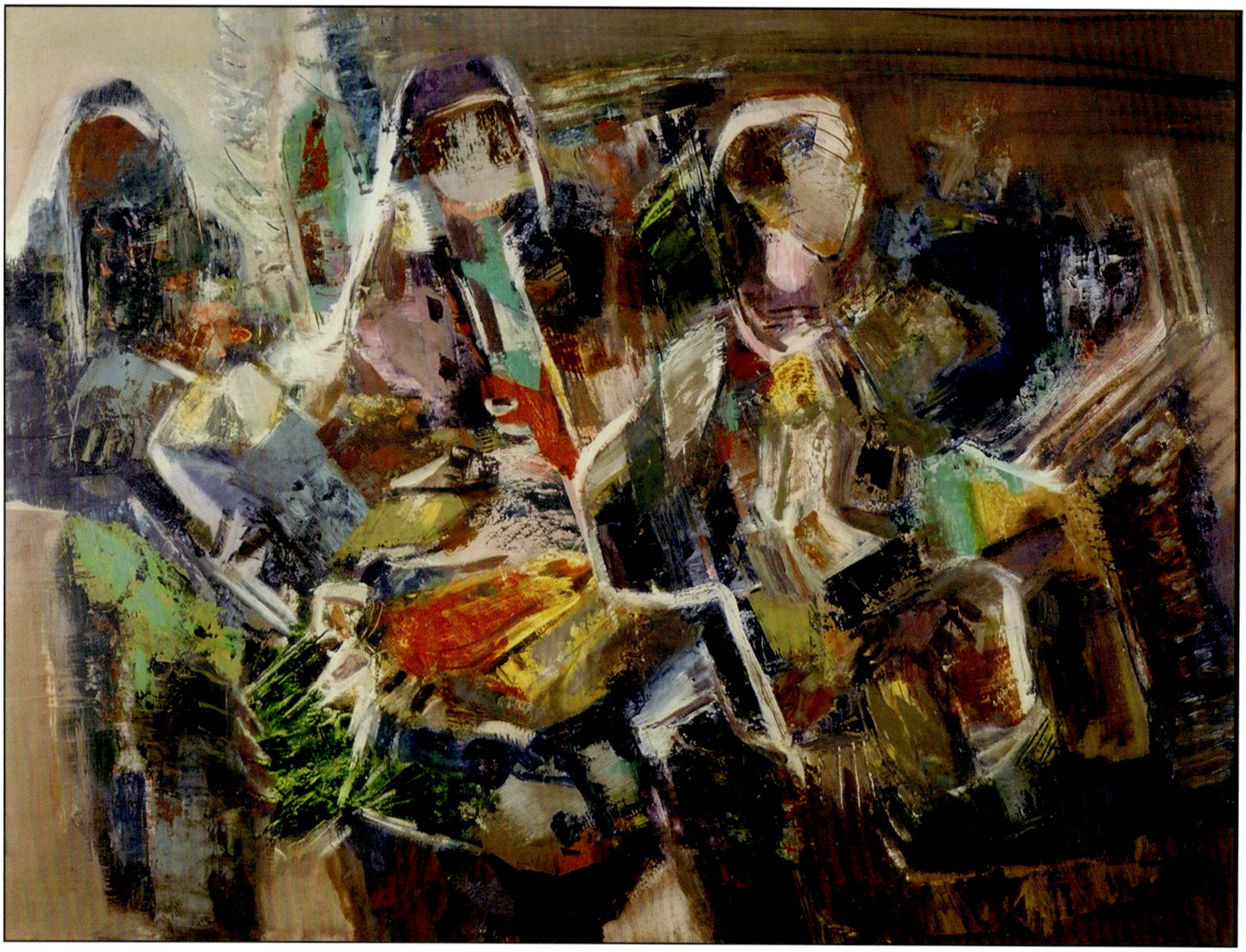

Actors/Three Actors. Oil on composition board. 1964, Adelaide. 91.5 x 122.0 cm. Estate of the artist. Photograph: Graeme Hastwell.

One of his best semi-abstracts in terms of the combinations of colours and textures, this painting shows that by this stage of his development Wlad had arrived at a highly individual conception in his figurative painting.

Festival Scenes Series, 1962-64

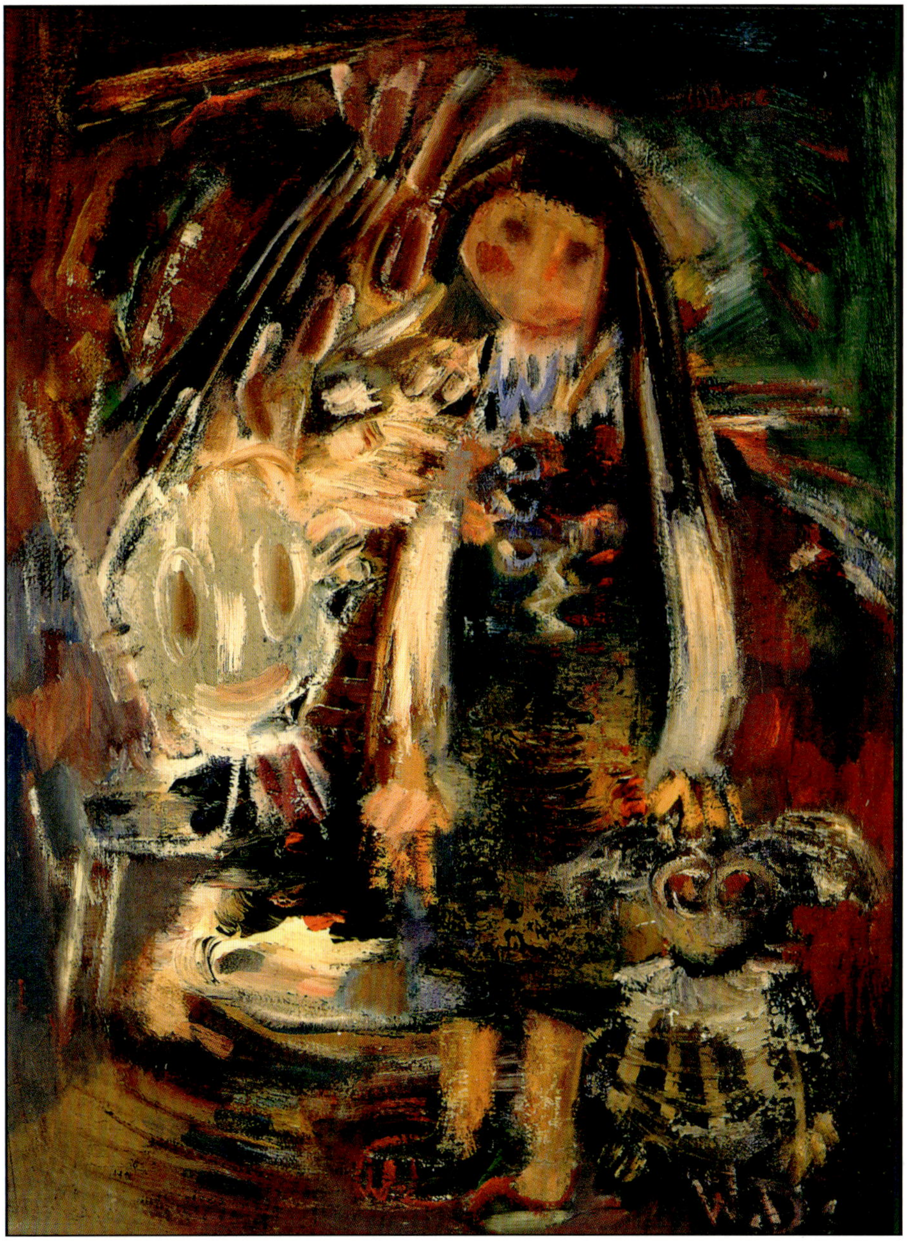

Ursula's Toy. Oil on canvas. ca.1964, Adelaide. 88.9 x 66.0 cm. Private collection, New South Wales. Photograph: Graeme Hastwell.

One of two versions of this subject, this painting is rendered with more brushwork whereas the other version is constructed predominately with palette knives and scrapers. Wlad continued to produce a number of felt pen drawings of his children with their friends or mother and other paintings on this theme throughout the decade.

Family Scenes Series, 1964-68

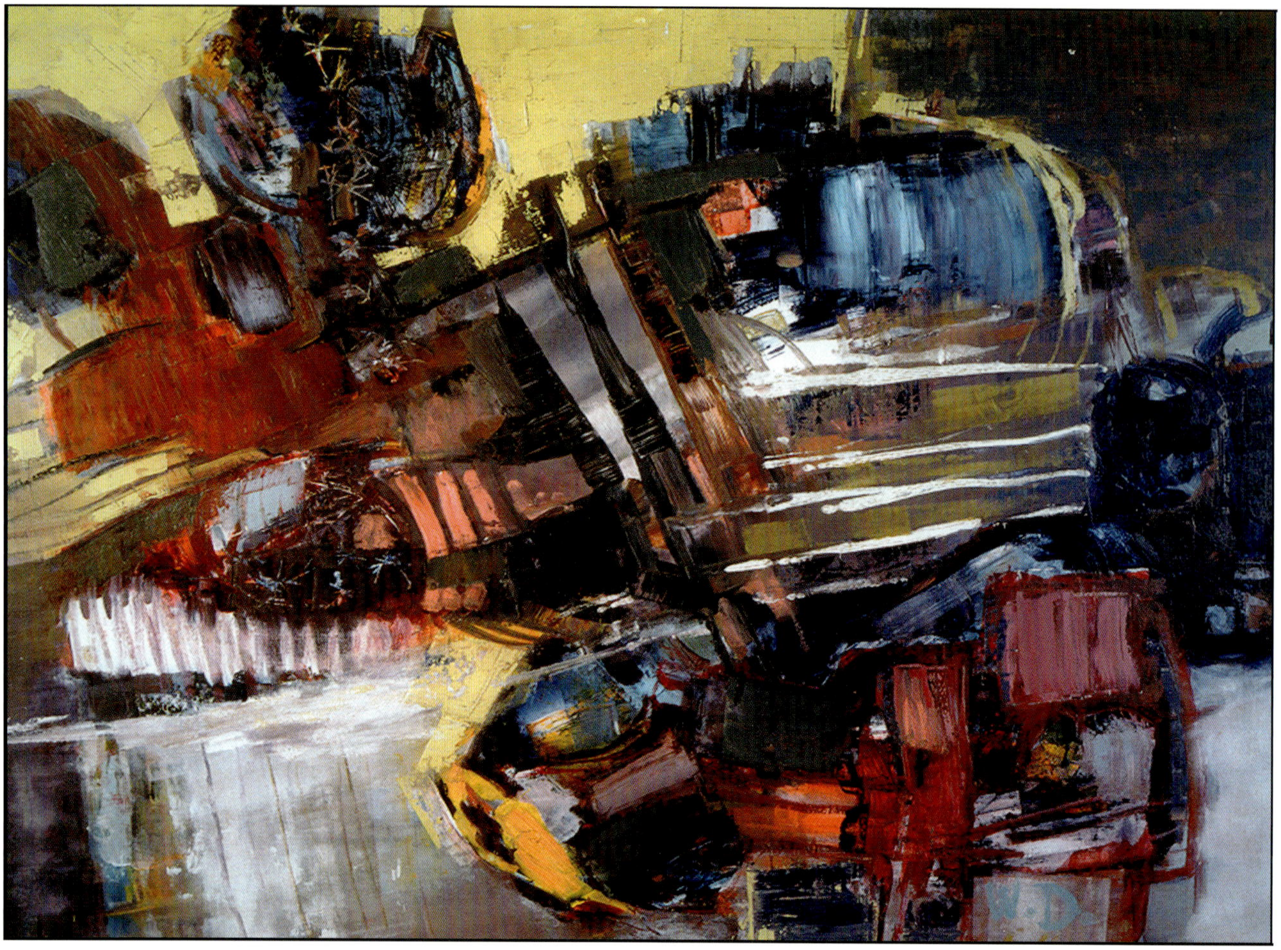

Yellow Fragment. Oil on composition board. 1962, Adelaide. 91.5 x 120.5 cm. Private collection, Sydney.
Photograph: Graeme Hastwell.

This is one of the most intriguing paintings of the era, full of fascinating details and textures, some applied by rollers, and enigmatic in conception. It seems to depict an apocalyptic landscape, littered with shards of glass and wrangled metal and an expanse of dark water, under a golden sky. True to some of his best paintings, its full encryption is clear only after considerable contemplation. One can ask, for instance, is there a map of Australia at top left centre, divided by a barbed wire fence, and why has he painted it? One can perhaps conclude that it contains a topical, political comment about the ever-looming shadow of the so-called "Yellow Peril," or perhaps the reality of atomic power and the impending problems posed by "yellow cake." Such narrative ambiguity is one of the picture's strengths, as it provides room for our imagination to roam, to speculate and to interrogate the forms, shadows and meanings. Similar techniques and imagery were explored in his series of abstracts based on the horror of the *Voyager* disaster in 1964.

Current Affairs & The Voyager Disaster Series, 1962-64

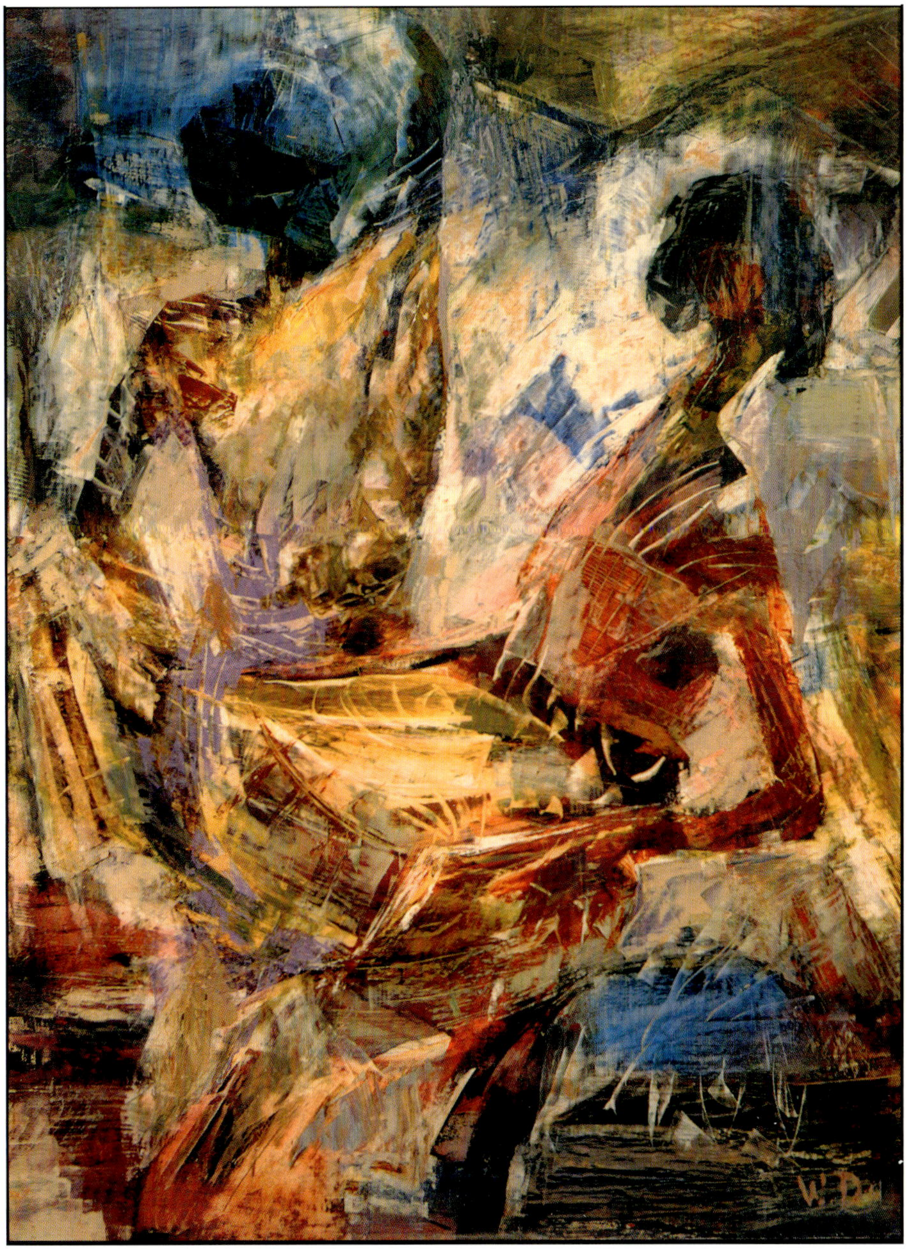

Grapepickers. Oil on composition board. 1966, Adelaide. 119.0 x 89.0 cm. Private collection, New South Wales. Photograph: Graeme Hastwell.

Here the artist relies entirely on scrapers and palette knives, resulting in a highly individual modernist conception of painting the figure, informed by his drawings of Aborigines and the ballet. The idea for this series came from a felt pen and coloured ink or watercolour submission for a mural commission in the Barossa Valley.

Vineyards Series, 1966

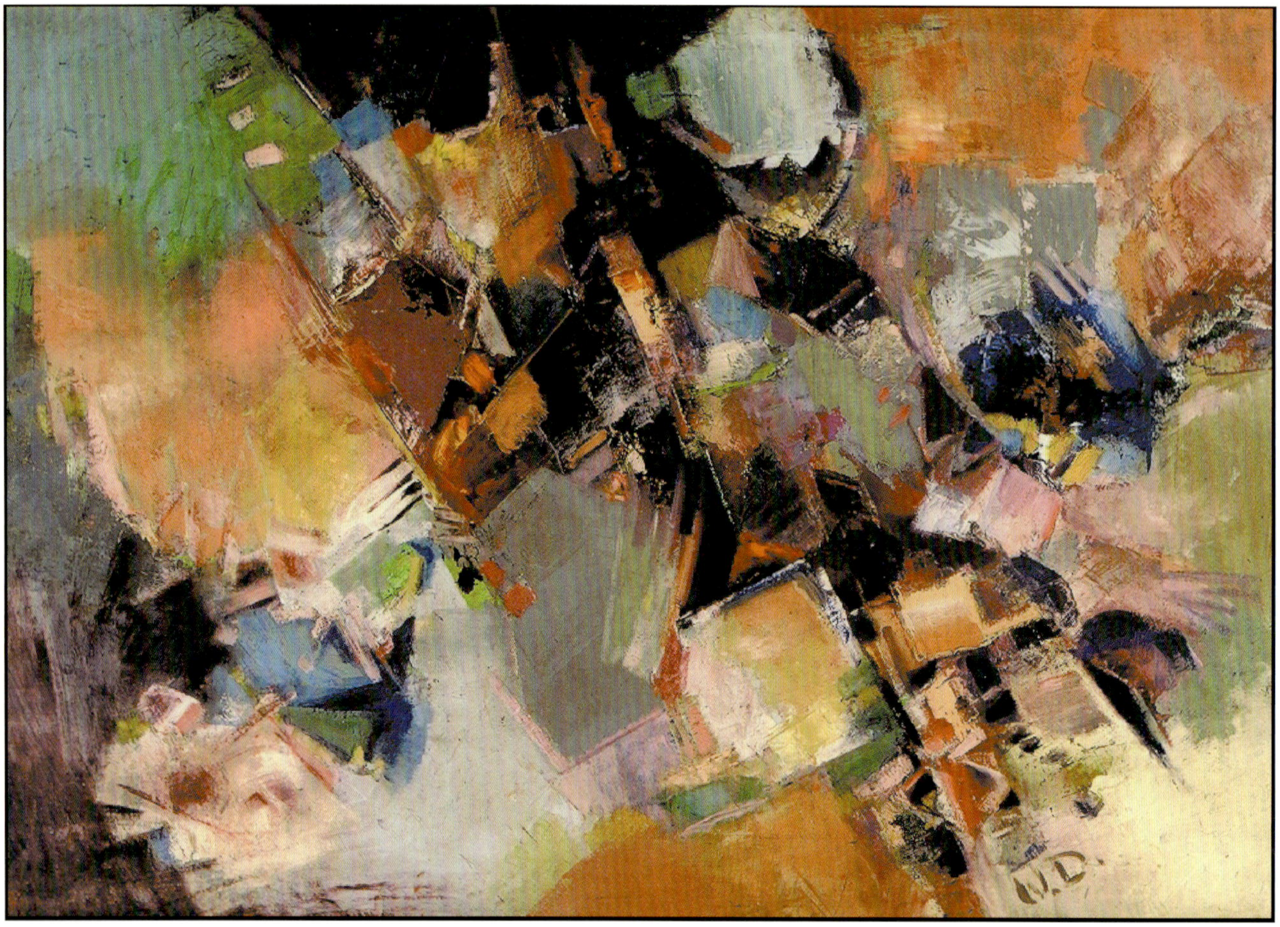

Opal gazer. 1965 Adelaide. Oil on composition board. 89.0 x 128.0 cm. Private collection, Melbourne.
Photograph: Graeme Hastwell.

Drilling through unyielding rock, the opal miner in the dusty centre of the continent seeks a glimpse of elusive opalescence. This work might be a metaphor for the 99% of hard work and perspiration that goes with Wlad's experimental method and into each mental "excavation". A smaller oil on canvas in green/blue palette from this series is in the collection of the Art Gallery of South Australia.

Opal Field Series, 1965

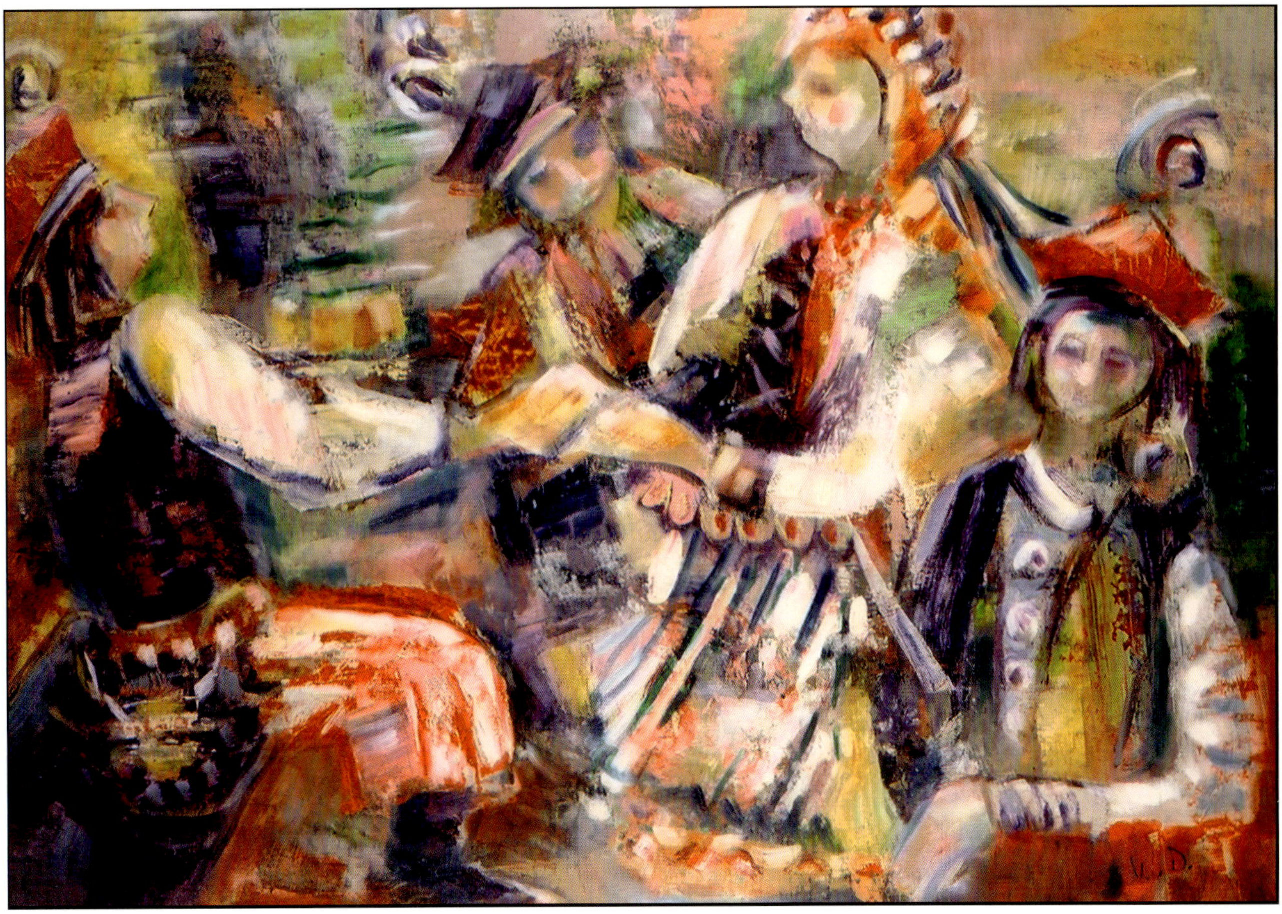

Mazowsze/Polish dancers. Oil on composition board. ca.1967, Adelaide. approx. 90.0 x 120.0 cm.
Private collection, Port Elliot. Photograph: Graeme Hastwell.

A superb painting of the Polish folk dancers from the Krakow region, full of sentiment and *joie de vie*, with delicate colouration and a sense of movement intricately woven into the composition. This is one of only several paintings on this theme, but there were numerous felt pen drawings in this series. This series was a natural extension of a previous series on the Chinese theatre (ca.1955), and Bolshoi ballet (1962), which to a large degree concentrated on paintings and colour or black and white felt pen drawings of Igor Stravinsky's ballet *Petrushka,* and *Swan Lake*. He completed a triptych on such themes in more spontaneous style for the Dom Polski Centre in Adelaide.

Mazowsze Series, 1967

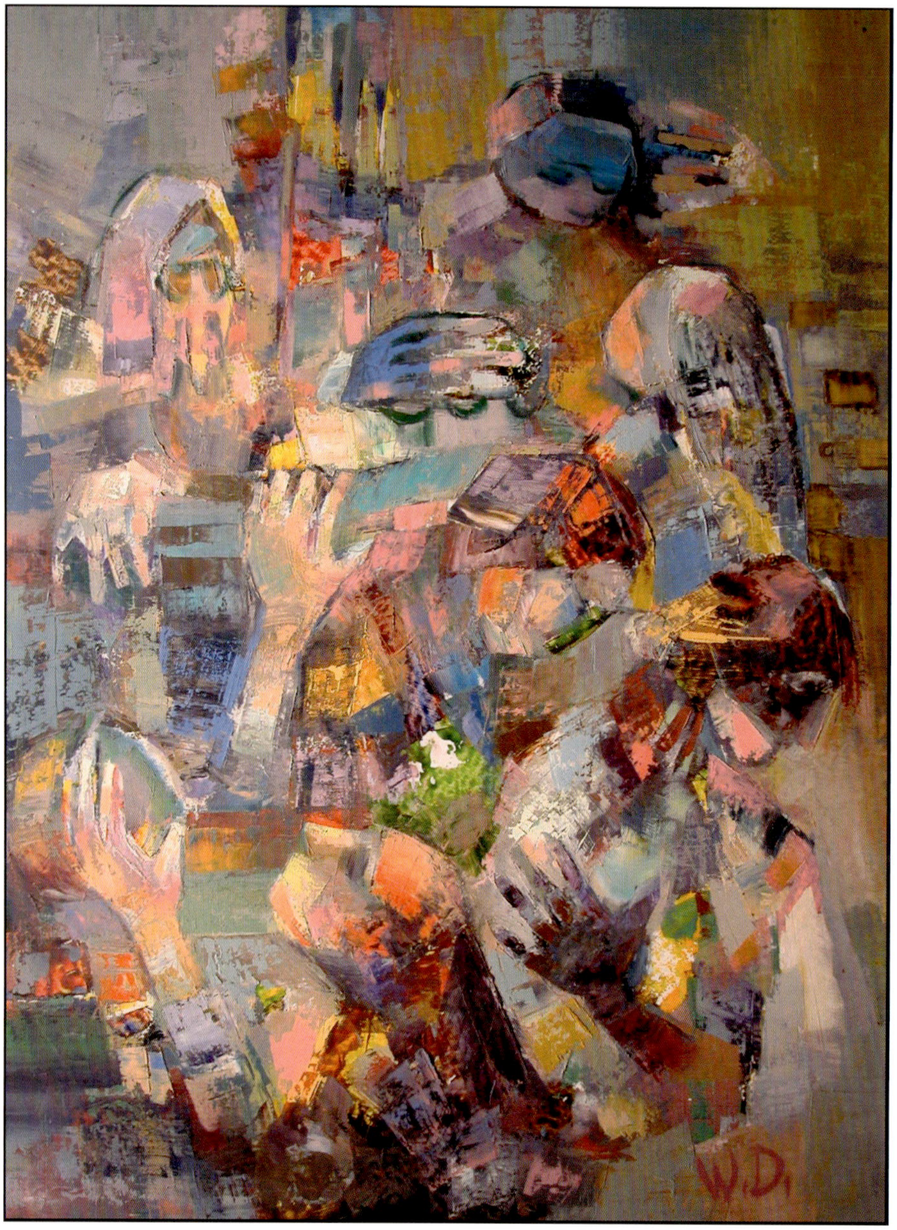

Protest. Oil on composition board. ca.1968, Adelaide. Private collection. 120.0 x 90.0 cm. Photograph courtesy Elder Fine Art, Adelaide.

One of the best emotionally charged figurative works of the late 1960s' period, it combines subtle colours and textures with theatrical gestures. The gestures of the figures link back to the powerfully expressive painting *Juggler* (1965), which almost won the Maude Vizard Wholohan Prize in 1966. This and another superb oil, *Party*, modelled on the watercolour *Beatniks* (p. 23), signified the artist's emergence from a bleak period dating from 1966, from which time the artist immersed himself in a palette of greys. A significant series of felt pen drawings also accompanied this series, showing youths in milk bars, playing Prosh Day pranks, in court rooms, window shopping or idling at the beach and in parks.

Youth of Today Series, 1968

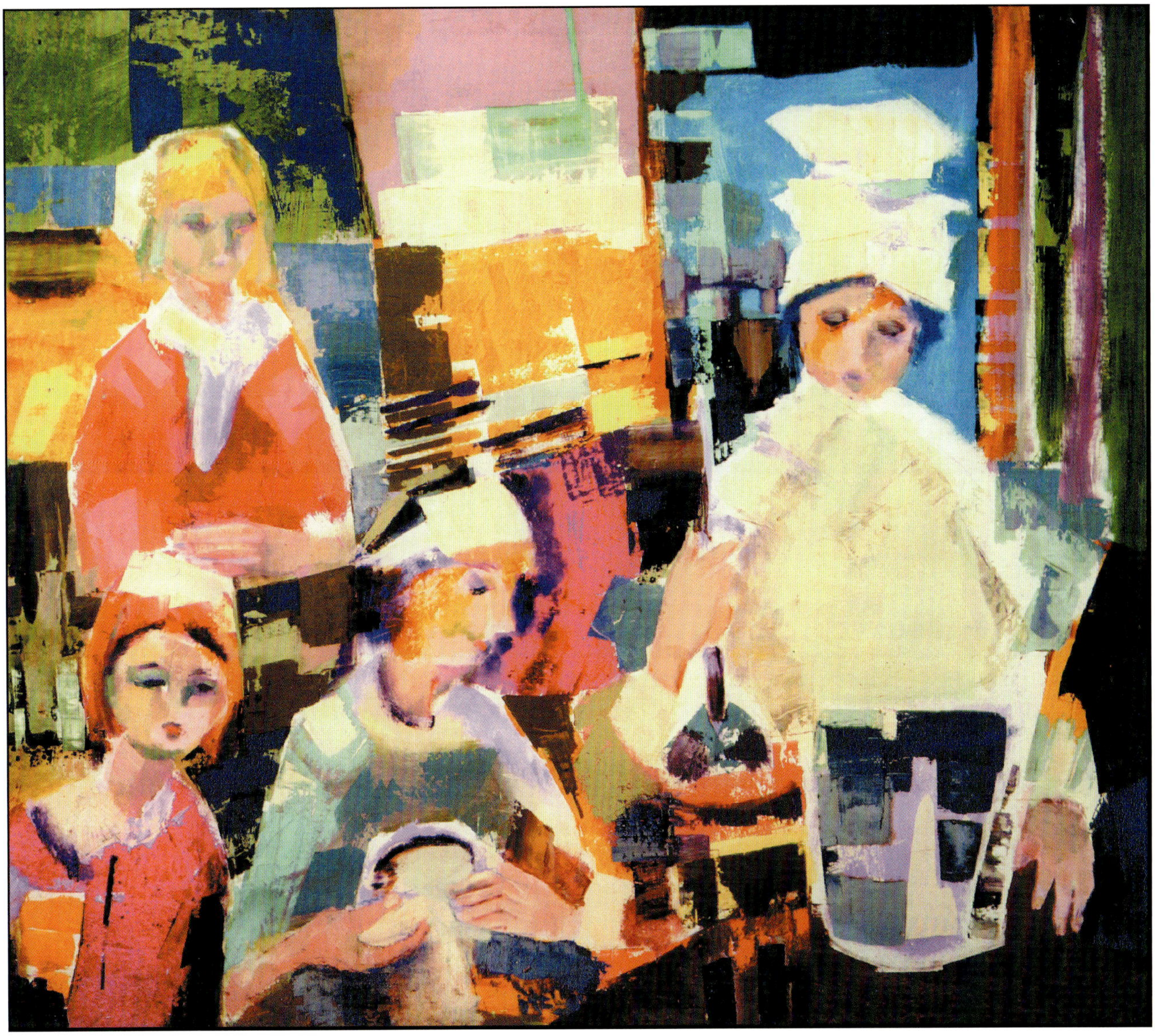

Kitchen. Oil on composition board. ca.1970, Adelaide. 122.5 x 137.5 cm. Estate of the artist.
Photograph: Graeme Hastwell.

Here the scraper technique of *Grapepickers* and *Protest* is simplified, like some of his abstracts at that time, such as *Piccadilly Valley*, with a brighter palette seemingly responding to Colour-Field painting and Pop Art of the time. The subject is more closely observed, and rendered in a style more finely attuned to his felt pen drawings for this series. He did a few other paintings of this scale and several others half-sized in the series, as well as a comprehensive number of drawings.

Hospital Series, 1970

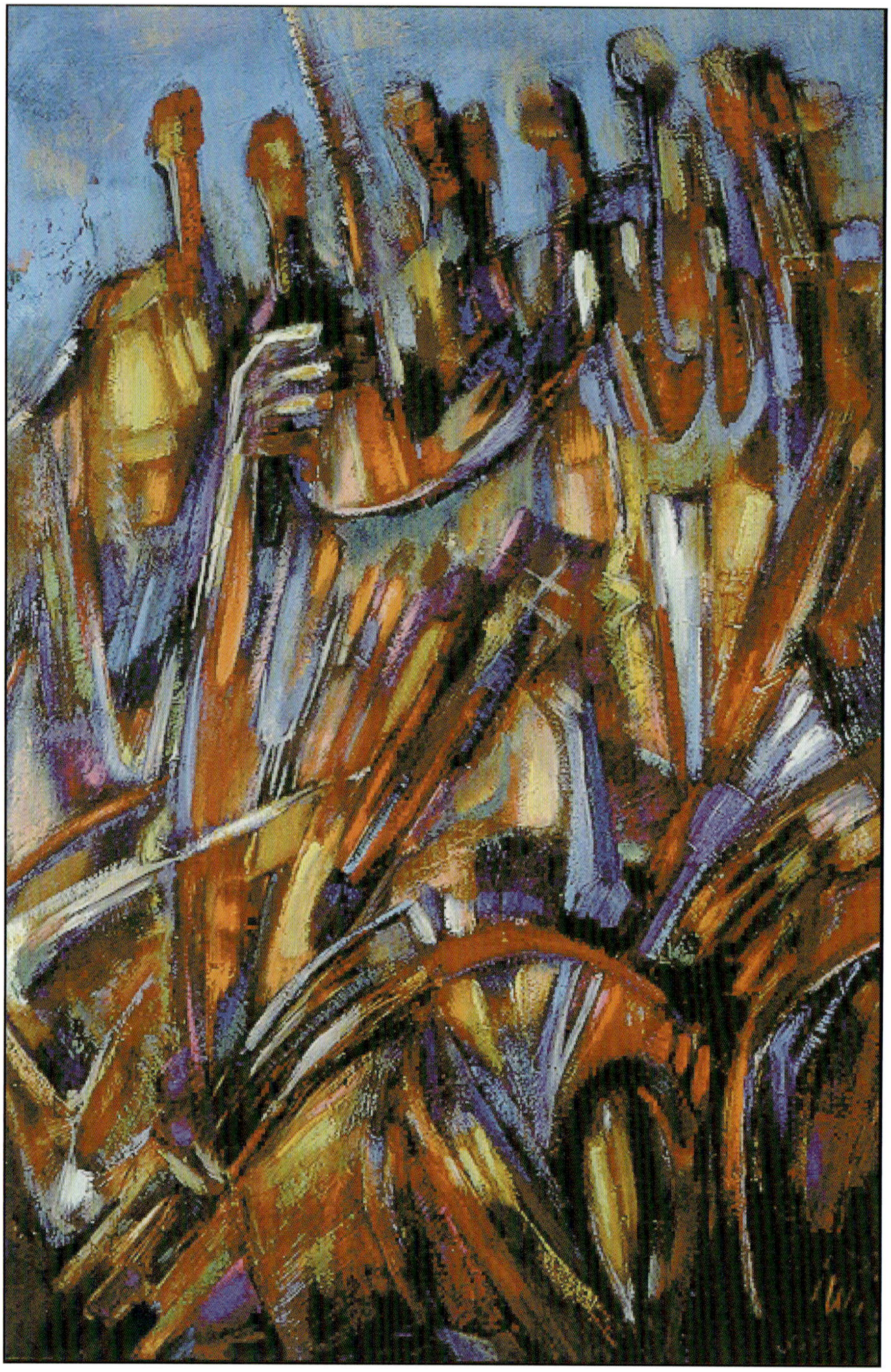

Dance. Oil on composition board. 1972, Adelaide. 91.5 x 61.0 cm. Private collection, Adelaide. Photograph: Graeme Hastwell.

Harking back to the abstracted figuration of the mid 1950s and early 1960s, based on Aboriginal figures, this painting is energised by rhythmic brushwork and superbly modulated organic tones and textures.

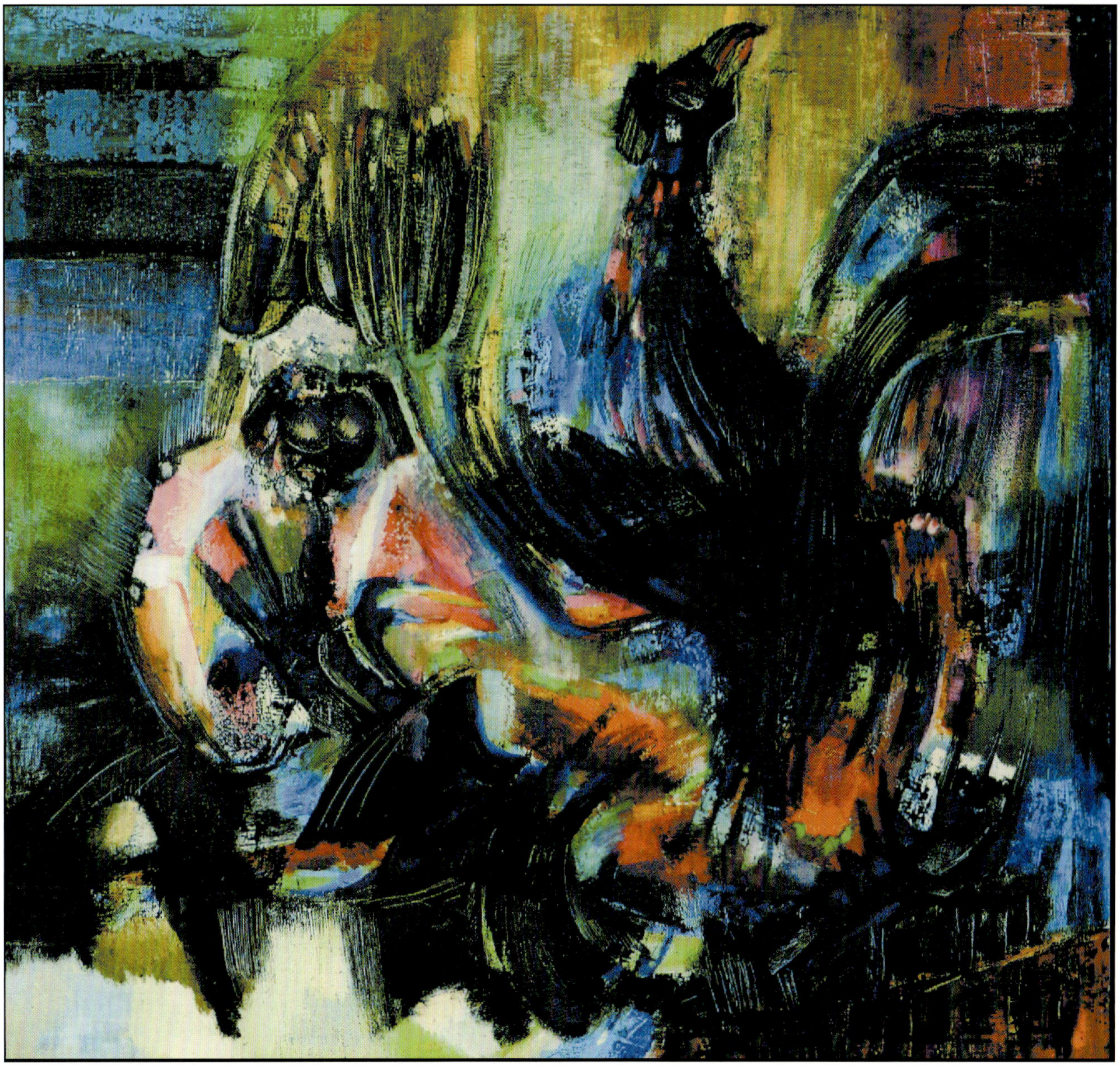

Phoenix Rising. Oil on canvas. 1972, Adelaide. 122.0 x 129.5 cm. Private collection, Adelaide. Photograph: Graeme Hastwell.

Another Aboriginal inspired work, it alludes seemingly to the resurrection of Indigenous culture in the early 1970s. I recall that he painted two other pictures featuring brolgas and cranes in similar gesture in this series, as well as one of Papuan warriors in their ceremonial headdress of Bird of Paradise feathers (reproduced in black and white on p. 58).

Indigenous Series, early 1970s

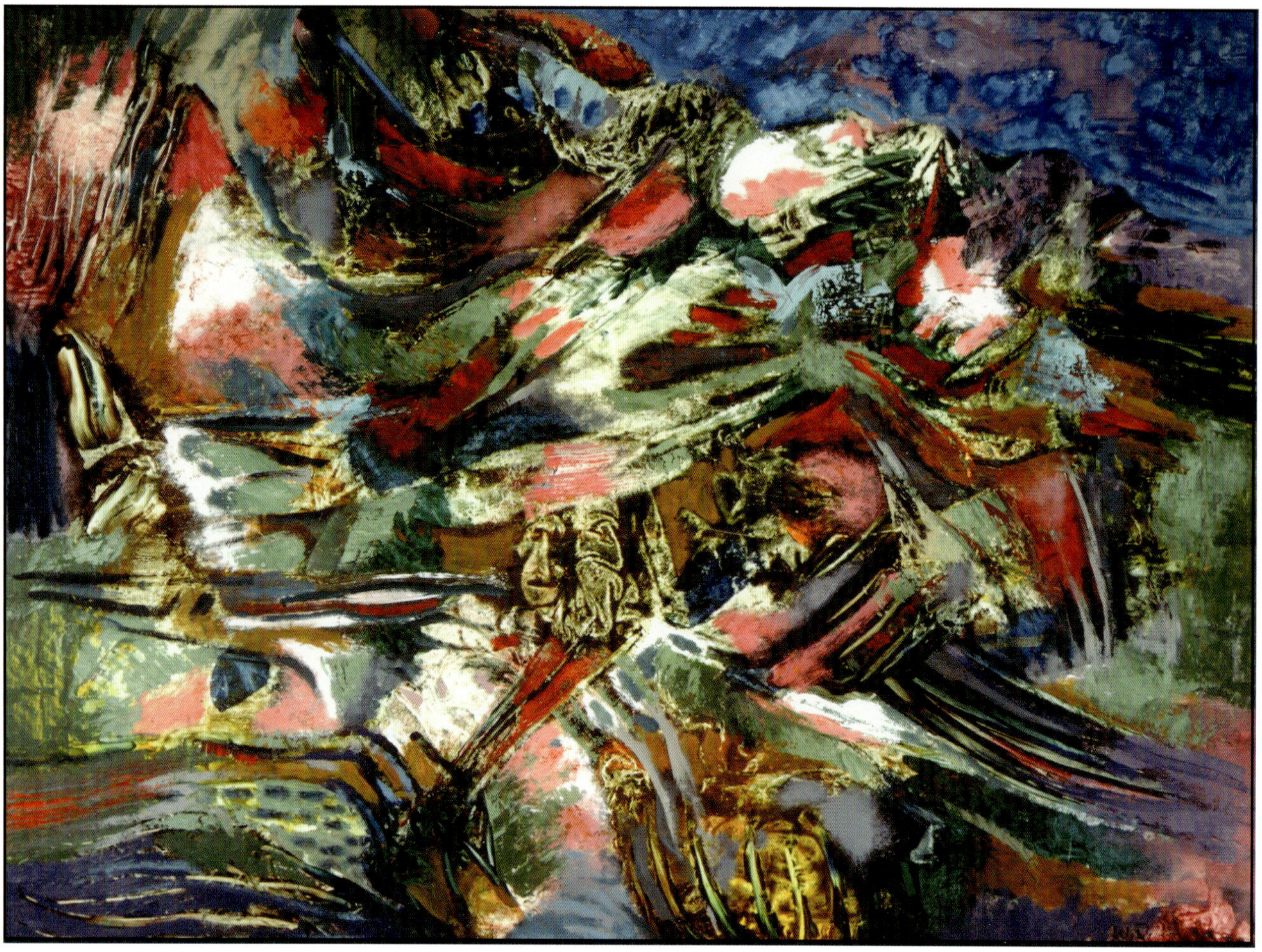

Tower Hill. Oil on composition board. ca.1975, Adelaide. approx. 90.0 x 120.0 cm. Private collection, Adelaide. Photograph: Graeme Hastwell.

A complex but slightly relaxed composition of profound subtlety in colour, texture and movement. The abstracted landscape is crammed with organic textures in its brass-toned palette. Triggered by a key brushstroke of vivid orange in its lower centre, a summoning up of magma from the site's volcanic origins, in concert with a seemingly incongruous and at first glance clumsy series of horizontal dark brushstrokes lower left, one tends to fall into the painting. I was astonished to find when I visited the site myself that this painting, more than any other, reveals the extent of Wlad's photographic memory and his artistic skill. I relived the painting as I moved down a hill past basalt, granite boulders, lichen and grasses towards a lake with a blue, sunlit, cloudy sky reflected in it. I realized that not only had he captured the colours, textures and tone of the place, but also had brilliantly evoked the prehistoric quality of the geography, geology, and the botany of the site.

Australia 1974-1975 Series

Brian Claridge

An Explication of Wladyslaw Dutkiewicz's Theory of Space-Time painting (ca.1955)

Introduction

The Polish-Australian artist, Wladyslaw Dutkiewicz, has developed his own particular form of expression. Two things were responsible for this. The first was the desire to escape the direct influence of any previous master, and not to merely continue to exploit an idiom already established. The second was the belief that there must be a way by which an artist can keep working without having to wait for his inspiration to suddenly happen – that he should not have to rely on the good fortune of a heaven-sent inspiration, but should be able to discover inspiration for himself by working with this in view.

An account of the method of working that Wladyslaw Dutkiewicz evolved as a result of these impulses is included in this paper.

There are two important consequences of this method outlined.

One is that a most significant expression has resulted which I believe is a definite and important contribution to art.

The artist has achieved, in those of his paintings which are so far based entirely on the method, work that must take its place in world art as advancing beyond the so far accepted artistic expressions.

The other point that emerges is the possibility that this method as applied to painting is a particular aspect of a more general inception that will have applications in other arts and other fields of thought. It is this possibility in which we are now interested. This is suggested at the end of the paper.

So far, tentative experiments have been made in music and poetry, and with sculptural and architectural forms, with encouraging results. I cannot help feeling that it is significant that, with Wladyslaw Dutkiewicz expressing his ideas purely in the terms of a painter, he has been able to give to non-painters the suggestion of a new approach in their own work (architecture in one case, music and poetry). This must mean that, somehow, he has been able to communicate through particular terms a more general conception.

Although this has not actually been expressed, it has, nevertheless, been intuitively grasped and worked upon. This strongly points to the possibility of there being a more general and fundamental expression of his idea that, once formulated, could prove useful in many other fields of activity.

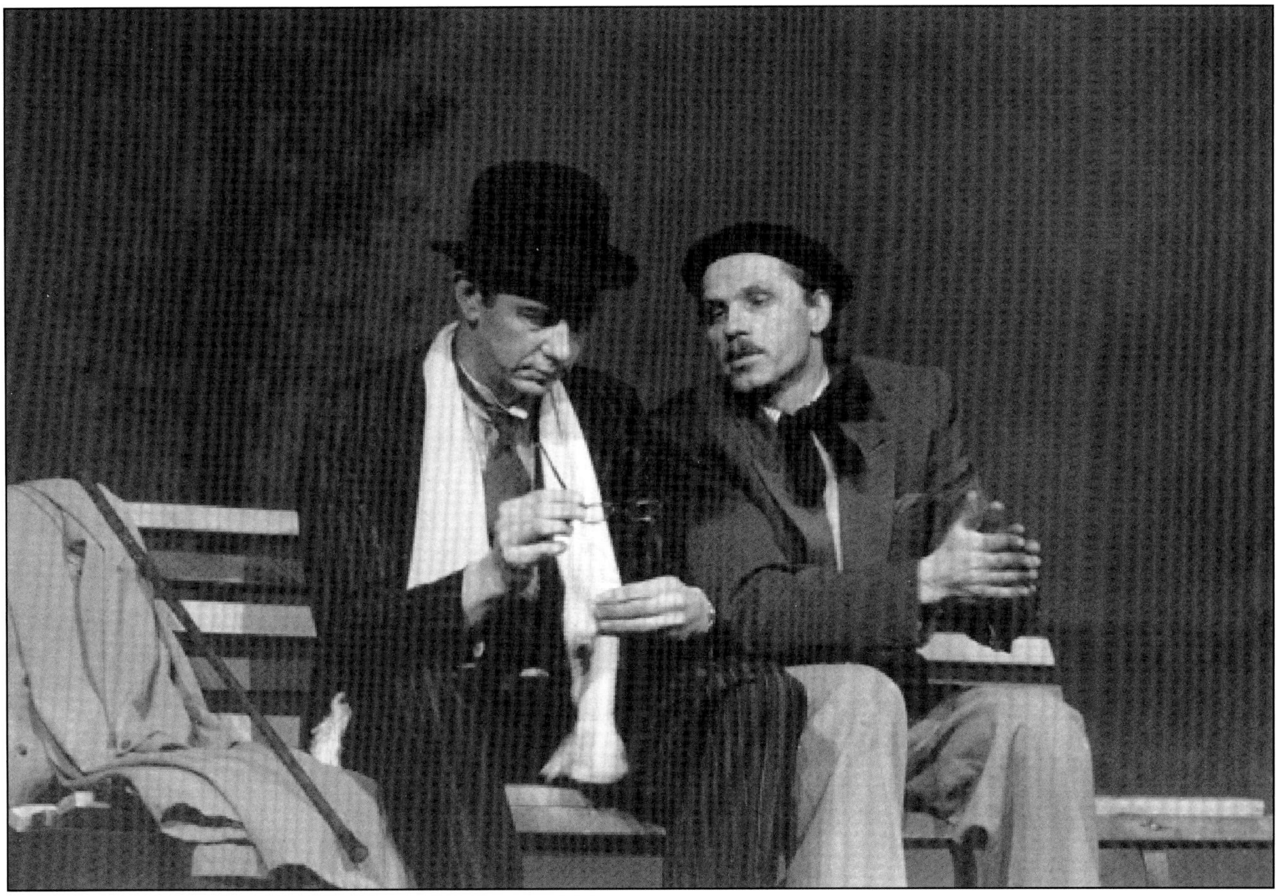

Brian Claridge and Wladyslaw Dutkiewicz performing in Dutkiewicz's production of Jean Jacques Bernard's *The Unquiet Spirit* for the Adelaide University Theatre Guild, Union Hall, Adelaide, 1959. Production photograph: Ian Davidson. Dutkiewicz Archive, State Library of South Australia/The Papers of Ian Davidson, Barr Smith Library.

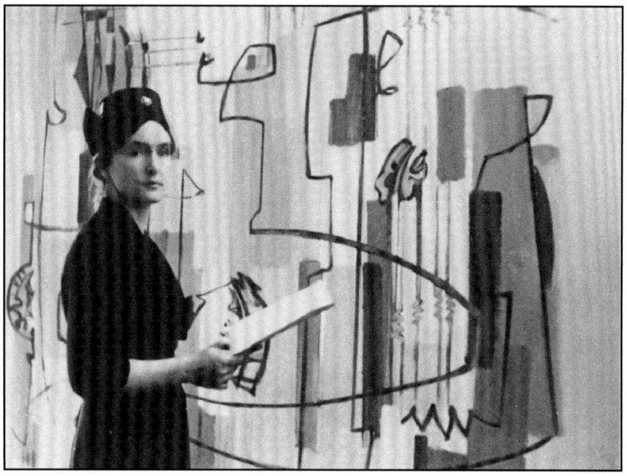

Nancy Claridge in front of mural, Claridge residence, Stonyfell. ca. early 1950s, Adelaide. Black and white photograph. Dutkiewicz Archive. Photograph: Ian Davidson.

On Wladyslaw Dutkiewicz's Theory

The role of the artist is to establish relationships between man and his world – to make new realms of feeling accessible – to give an emotional significance to aspects of our life that normally lack it.

This has been done by artistic methods which have been derived from the physical appearance of our world, or from the scientific knowledge that attempts to explain it, or has been done simply by intuition.

Further, the art of any era has only made real contributions toward establishing new relationships between man and his world when the methods have been consistent with the thought and knowledge of the time.

These methods, however, have always given rise to forms of expression in terms of man himself – man as existing in space and time interpreting other things and phenomena existing in space and time. Art has never appeared to seek further than this, although there have been philosophical suggestions that our experience of the world does not represent the true nature of things. This view has developed from Kant, who maintained that space and its characteristics and time are products of our consciousness. The placing of things in space and time exists only in us, and not in the things themselves.

No form of artistic expression has taken such ideas into account. Since the beginning of this century when these ideas, first suggested by Kant, were at last taken up by others, modern art, too, has developed forms of expression in terms of man himself – not in terms of man outside himself.

One of the last and most important statements in art considered to be in line with today's thought and knowledge is that of the Cubists. This appears to be consistent with the new space-time conception described by Einstein and Minkowski[1] with the simultaneous representation of various aspects of the one object, regarded as an artistic parallel to the ideas of relativity. We can no longer think it possible to fully describe an object from a single point of reference – a moving point of reference is necessary to fully comprehend an object.

But the cubist approach – the simultaneous representation of several facets of the object or group of objects is really just as inadequate as the single aspect represented by classical perspective. The cubist statement, from two or three, or even a hundred points of reference, all still with a definite relationship to the object, falls as far short of the infinite number of random points of reference suggested by the notion of relativity as does the single aspect presented by classical perspective. The cubist attempt to achieve full description now appears naive and inadequate. It can be regarded only as a first approximation – nevertheless an important one – to an art form fully parallel to our new space-time conception.

In the developments of cubism which were purely abstract, with no reference to any specific object, the art possesses no qualities in any way related to this conception. The moment the object is abandoned, the cubist approach loses its true and original significance. We find the artists returning to colour and texture, as, without the object, they have nothing to say other than in colour and form harmonies.

Of the artists concerned with abstract art and not connected with the cubists, Kandinsky stands as most important, and something of a prophet. In his writing as well as in his painting, he tried to establish the principles of artistic harmony and counter-point, and was concerned with the psychic effect of forms on man. He abandoned objective painting in favour of abstract because he feared obscuring pure art by the emotions aroused by objects. He loved "only form that comes of necessity from the spirit, and had been created by the spirit". He maintained that "the Philosophy of Art will in the future study with particular attention the spirit of things as well as their physical existence – an atmosphere will be created which will enable the human race to feel this spirit in the same unthinking way it now appreciates external appearance – and through this, the spirit of matter and finally the spirit of the abstract will become quite evident to humanity. From this new faculty will spring the joy of pure abstract art."[2]

Here is the suggestion that there will come an artistic expression which is derived from consideration of things outside of man and his space-time world – that art will be animated by the "spirit of things" – not of particular things, but of all things – rather than by their outward appearance.

Kandinsky, though sensing the future course of art, did not himself go beyond the "musical" aspect of art, his

[1] "A mathematical formulation of the special theory of relativity was given by Minkowski. It is based on the idea that an event is specified by four coordinates, three spatial coordinates and one time coordinate. These coordinates define a four-dimensional space and the motion of a particle can be described by a curve in this space, which is called Minkowski space-time ... In special relativity the motion of a particle that is not acted upon by any forces is represented by a straight line in Minkowski space-time." In Valerie H. Pitt (ed.), *The Penguin Dictionary of Physics*, (Penguin, 1977).

[2] Although there have been numerous translations over time, this quote is presumably taken from a contemporary edition of Kandinsky's *Concerning the Spiritual in Art*.

expression being based on the intuitive harmonies, rhythms and counterpoints of lines, colours and forms which comprise his Compositions.

Just at the time that Kandinsky was working and thinking in this direction, the challenge of Kant was again being taken up, and a first understanding of the problem he posed becomes evident. A new approach to the problem of space and time involving the conception of "the fourth dimension" appears.

Kant asserted that everything known to us through the senses is known in terms of space and time, and, by the senses, we know nothing outside of space and time. Kant established the fact that extension in space and existence in time are not properties belonging to things, but are just the properties of our sensuous receptivity. In reality, apart from our sensuous knowledge of things, they exist independently of space and time. Perceiving things sensuously we impose upon them the conditions of space and time. Space and time, then, do not represent properties of the world, but are properties of our knowledge of the world which, in reality, has neither extension in space or existence in time. We require these aids for perceiving the world. A thing having no definite extension in space or existence in time has virtually no meaning for us. A thing not in space will not differ from any other thing in any particular, and may occupy the same place simultaneously with any other thing. And all phenomena not in time – not regarded in relation to past, present, and future – would co-exist for us simultaneously. Our consciousness isolates things for us into categories of space and time, but the division exists only in us and in our knowledge of things, and not in the things themselves.

Kant left the problem here, suggesting we could never know the real thing itself outside of space and time by nature of our psychic make-up. Schopenhauer, however, suggested we could, through intuition. Later suggestions are that it is possible to develop a higher psychic constitution which will enable us to really know things as they exist independently of space and time. This is the thought based on the conception of the "fourth dimension".

This assertion of the existence of things outside of man's perception of them – in no relation to the man-imposed divisions of space and time – is suggestive of Kandinsky's idea of the spiritual aspect of things which he predicted would be the concern of the art of the future, and which goes beyond the mere physical appearance of things.

This leads to an art form in which the expression is not in terms of man himself and his sensuous knowledge of the world, but rather an expression which acknowledges the existence of things in themselves, outside of man. Such expression will result in the creation of new forms which will be derived from the discoveries of a consciousness roaming freely outside the limitations of space and time.

The new forms will exist in their own right, without reference to man's sensuous knowledge of the world, without any particular reference to how man perceives the objective world, or how science suggests he might see it. The forms will be universally valid as regards the observer's position in space and time. This, incidentally, will represent the true parallel between an artistic expression and the philosophical and scientific knowledge of our time.

The artistic forms will appear in a way similar to that which may be considered to be the way things, outside of man's knowledge of them, have come to exist.

The art of Wladyslaw Dutkiewicz is an expression of this kind. It is an art form that takes man outside of himself. It is a first realization of Kandinsky's prophecy. Forms result from an understanding of the independent existence of things.

The method W.D. has evolved was arrived at purely intuitively from the desire to produce paintings in a manner entirely new, and which were in no way derived from the methods so far employed.

Wladyslaw Dutkiewicz starts with a series of arbitrarily chosen points in space, inside or outside the limits of the canvas. These are in no particular relationship to each other or to the artist. From any point to any other, pairs of lines are drawn completely freely, spontaneously, the hand guiding, not the mind. And so a kind of network is evolved upon the canvas, and from the intersecting lines, certain shapes and lines are chosen and consciously developed or refined, according to the artist's aesthetic.

Further, between each pair of lines is imagined and applied a colour, extending between the lines from point to point. Where the pairs of lines cross other pairs, so, too, do the colours. So new colours are born within the intersections in the same way as the shapes between the intersections are discovered. By this method colour and shape are thus two organic elements which cannot be regarded as separate, but only as an indivisible unity – they are born as one, together.

This represents the primary exercise, whereby the idea of organizing and choosing shapes and forms is developed consciously. These shapes are still essentially flat – only two dimensional. Shapes so discovered may now take their place amongst other points and other discovered shapes, and again, by the same process, further organization is possible. New shapes are discovered out of the old in an organic manner by a continuous process. But now the colours and disposition of the shapes develops a spatial quality which the first flat organization of initial shapes lacked. Further, this spatial quality is in a constant state of movement, for it is related to no specific view point or horizon. Nor is it related to any particular number of view points or perspective frames. The forms exist simultaneously in all space and in all time: they are viewed entirely outside space and time.

However, there is no reason why any previous convention should not be fused onto this method. But the important thing is that the method is in no way dependent upon them, and the most significant work is achieved when they are rejected.

NB. Claridge had no contact with the Constructivists of Sydney or beyond of this period and developed this paper from discussions with the artist, who then did not then have the facility with English to record his ideas.

Chronology

1918 Wladyslaw Wojciech Dutkiewicz is born into a difficult, rustic life in Stara Sol, near Lwow, Poland, on 21 February. As the third surviving son, he is expected to become a priest, and has been named after the first bishop of Poland, Wojciech, which was also the name of his father Michal's father, who is from a shoemaker's family and is a wood carver and sculptor of note. Michal was a soldier in the Austro-Hungarian army during WWI.

1920 Poland goes to war with Bolshevik Russia. The family home is once again situated in the middle of conflict. Wlad and his mother are lucky to survive. A Bolshevik revolutionary breaks down the door and threatens to kill the Polish family, holding a pistol up to the head of the infant as Maria holds him to her breast. Somehow the gun jams and the marauding revolutionary withdraws.

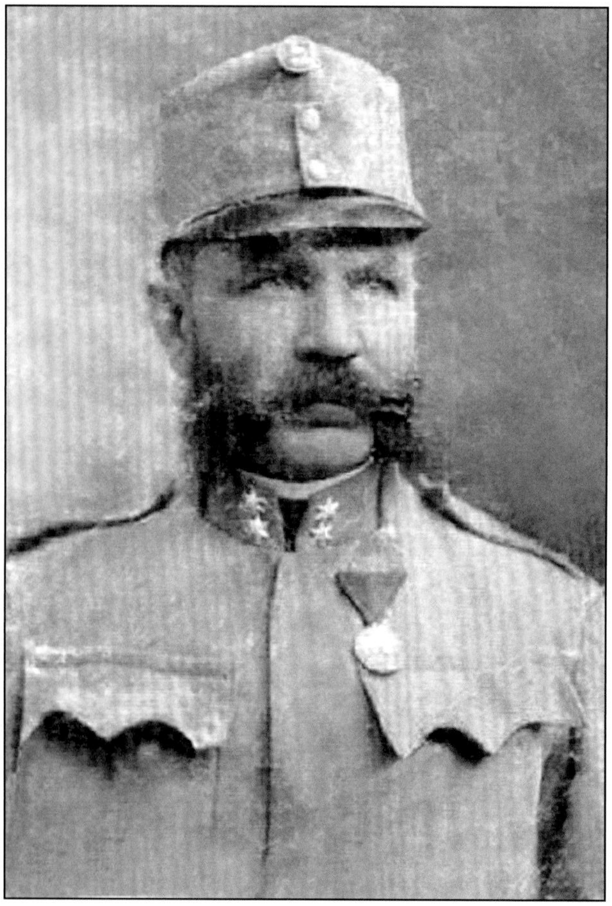

Michal Dutkiewicz, WWI. ca.1916, Galicia. Black and white photograph. Dutkiewicz Archive.

1923-24 Wlad demonstrates a lively intelligence and rare talent and begins school a couple of years earlier than most children. Initially he follows his older brothers in being educated at a village school. Wlad wakes at 5.30am each morning to serve as an altar boy in the local church, in preparation for his vocation as priest.

late 1920s Michal is educating older brother Jan as a painter and encouraging Wlad in the theatre. He takes him to see silent films at the Rialto cinema in Lwow. The boy is inspired by his favourite film stars, especially Charlie Chaplin and Greta Garbo, and he enjoys the Marx Brothers. The first two were great actors and wake Wlad to the possibilities of theatre. He holds his own plays at home and decides to participate in the school drama productions produced by Maria Kisiakiewicz. His first acting role is as Iwan Wasiliewicz Lomow in Anton Chekhov's *The Proposal*. On one occasion he plays the devil in a nativity play, and is so convincing he scares the wits out of the audience.

1928-32 The high school is located in Sambor, several miles to the north, and it is an adventure getting to school, for the children have to walk, whether in rain, snow or sunshine. The major holidays are in summer. Wlad is a creative midfielder and becomes captain in one of the local football teams. He continues as altar boy, and is a celebrity through his artistic talents. He plays cards and chess with his teachers, and is too clever to get punished by his elders for his misdemeanours, for he is recognized as a bit of a rascal by his peers and a number of neighbours.

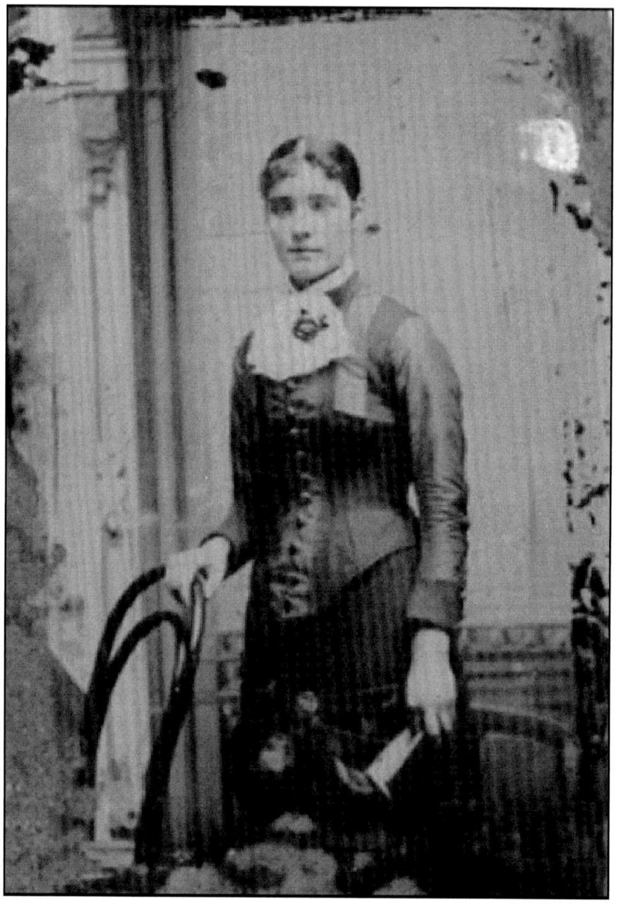

Maria Sas-Grzegorzewicz. ca.1900, Galicia. Tintype. Dutkiewicz Archive.

1932 His father, Michal, dies on Wlad's birthday, aged 54. He was summoned to rescue someone who had fallen through ice and also slipped into the icy water. He caught pneumonia and survived only three weeks. Wlad assumes his father's duties: he has to organize the farm, its slaughtering and harvests, and daily duties; and continues his studies part-time. He works for some time in the local salt pans.

1935 Wlad completes his last year of high school, which enables him to enter university. By then Jan is a postgraduate art student in Krakow. He manages to make an appointment for Wlad with his professor, Kazimierz Sichulski, who is regarded as the best teacher of drawing and the best political cartoonist of his era, in order to enter the academy in Krakow. The professor teaches Wlad for one year, ca.1935-36, and he grows to greatly respect his tutor.

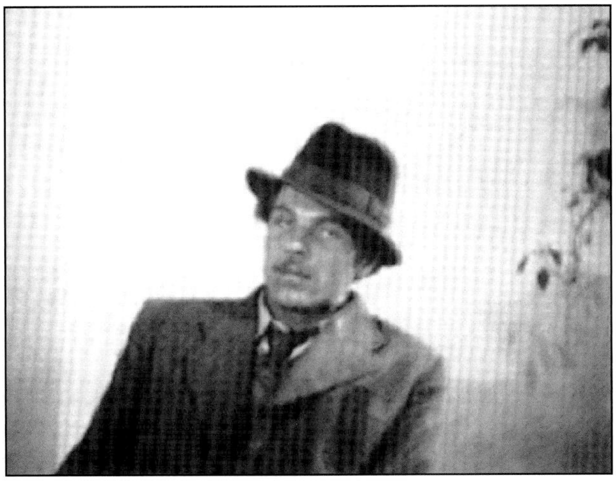

Wlad in Paris. Photograph. 1937, Paris. Dutkiewicz Archive.

1937 Wlad wins a government scholarship to study painting in Paris at *L'Ecole des Beaux Arts*. The scholarship pays only for fees and enrolment, so he works making roads with other foreign and local students, and as a waiter and bar attendant in restaurants and cafes. His knowledge of several languages becomes invaluable in cosmopolitan Paris. Wlad meets the great Russian-born bass-baritone, Feodor Shaliapin (b.1873, d.1938), the mime artist Marcel Marceau, and other painters, such as Utrillo and even Picasso, at a club near his flat in Montmartre, a haunt of intellectuals and artists centred in Paris.

1938 Wlad attends the Summer School in Landscape Painting, held by the Krakow Academy at the Carpathian mountain village of Zakopane. He deploys his comic skills to devise some much-needed Regulations to assist the students.

1939 Wlad is appointed as set designer for the Lwow Great Theatre (*Teatr Wielki*), taking classes at night in acting, directing and stage design, focussing on the theories of Constantin Stanislavsky.

1 September Germany invades Poland. Some of the academics from Krakow, including Jan and Professor Sichulski, have already moved ahead of the Nazi advance to Lwow. Wlad and Jan are enlisted into the Home Guard. Wlad works for Bereznecki's firm of housepainters and handymen. The firm is commissioned to refurbish houses, offices and churches, sometimes with mural and leadlight designs. Wlad becomes foreman and organizes the workers.

3 September The Nazis advance and within a few days cross the River Vistula and move into Krakow.

17 September The Soviets attack Eastern Poland. Wlad is shot by Russian soldiers, with five bullet wounds in right thigh, while trying to close the doors of Bernadine Church in Lwow, a headquarters for the Undergound. He is left for dead by soldiers, who do not enter the church. Jan emerges from the basement and saves him.

29 September The Government in Warsaw surrenders. Poland is partitioned. The next day General Sikorski sets up the Polish Government in Exile in Paris.

December With the release of Polish theatre workers to coincide with the installation of the Soviet regime in the territory, Wlad returns to the Great Theatre. He is asked by the Soviets to run the theatre and support is offered. He produces plays by Chekov and others. On one occasion the Opera is required to present Reinhold Moritzovitch Glière's *The Red Poppy* (1927), a ballet recounting a colourful story of the Russian fleet visiting China. Wlad commissions Jan to design the sets, with younger brother Ludwik assisting and performing. On opening night the Ukraine-born Nikita Khrushchev, the apparatchik who eventually succeeded Stalin after the war, visits the theatre amid much political pomp and ceremony. Wlad gains the Soviets' confidence and over time occasionally dares to present Polish nationalist pieces.

1940 Wlad and Jan continue to work for the Resistance under Professor Groer, forging papers for refugees and "wanted" Poles, whom they hide in the basement of their apartment until they can get them out. They send refugees to Romania, Yugoslavia, Hungary and in some appropriate cases the German Occupied Zone.

13 April Ludwik is prevented from boarding a train to return home to Stara Sol by an old school friend and is told his mother, Maria, youngest brother, Henryk, and younger sister, Cecylia, have been captured and deported to Aktiubinsk, Kazakhstan, NE of the Caspian Sea.

1 May Wlad is arrested and deported to Magnitogorsk in the lower Ural Mountains in Siberia, just north of Aktiubinsk, where Maria, Henryk and Cecylia are interred. He is regularly interrogated during his imprisonment of ten months. He tries to contact his family but fails.

1941 Wlad is flown back to Lwow to work as a propaganda artist. While he was away Jan had married Czeslawa, whose father was a railway signalman. She has skills as a radio operator and works with Jan in his Underground activities. Jan and Czeslawa make it clear that Wlad is to look after Ludwik. Wlad resumes resistance activities for several months. He and other trained artists work with *Sojuz Radianskich Chudoznikow*, an artists' collective. Some members of the collective, including Wlad and Ludwik, live together in a flat occupying the 3rd floor of 5 Paderewski Street, Lwow. SRC works from a large studio space in the city and attracts the attention of the authorities who put them to work for the propaganda ministry, painting *Polit Byuro* portraits. The enormous size of these portraits, which are used as billboards, necessitate new working methods. The artists adopt a production line with Wlad doing ears, Ludwik noses, Jan mouths and Zygmunt Lopuszynski (also a poet) eyes. They are so efficient they produce three at a time, enabling them to pursue other activities. But increasingly unrealistic deadlines force the artists to take rolled-up canvases home to their flat and to work on them at night. The finished portraits are inspected by a Selection Committee with a magnifying glass and any unacceptable detail is taken as a deliberate insult, or subversion, and pay is deducted. The pay becomes meagre and infrequent, barely enough to cover food and power bills.

22 June The Nazis attack the Soviets. There is intense fighting around Lwow. Wlad and Jan continue resistance activities, and most of the refugees they help are now Jews.

9 July Wlad is supplied with a form giving him the authority to buy paint and art materials, written in Russian and German. The Nazi authorities requisition his flat at 5 Paderewski Street. Professor Groer, a Jew, is arrested.

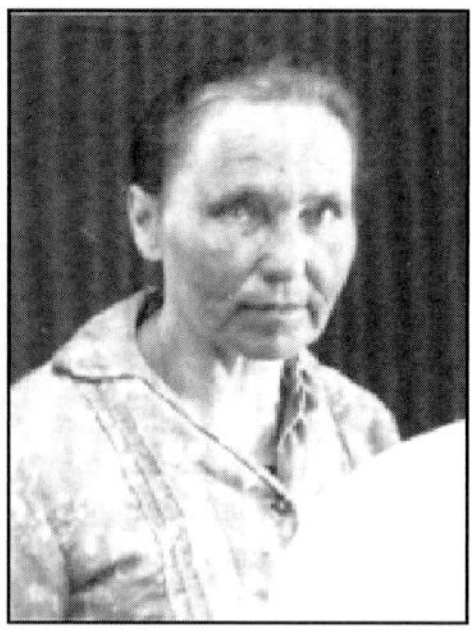
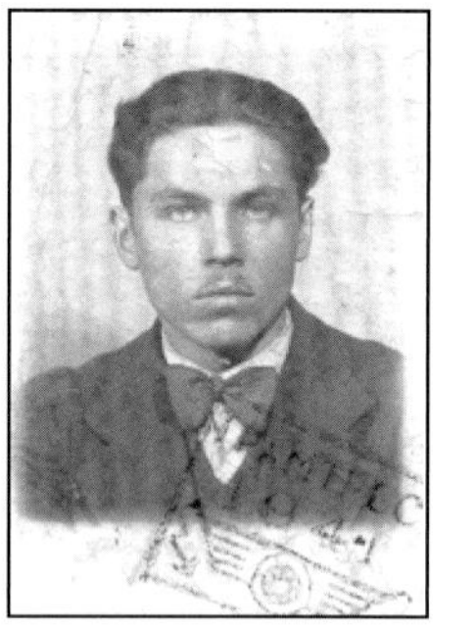

Maria and Wlad under Soviet rule, ca.1941. Two identity photographs. Dutkiewicz Archive.

15 October Wlad receives a retrenchment notice with two weeks' notice but gets good references which help him through the rest of the war.

16 November Wlad and Ludwik move to a flat on 3rd floor of 26 Batory Street. The Ukrainian Police had noted that Wlad had produced a play at the Great Theatre about the national hero the Polish general Tadeusz Kosciuszko and that he had introduced subtle patriotic symbols on the stage, so they move against him. He is arrested on the following day and taken to a concentration camp near Lwow (probably Janowska). The battle for Lwow continues until the Germans secure the region by December 1941. Wlad does not avoid the terror of war on account of his imprisonment, for he is sent to work for the *BauDienst*, a semi-military unit of conscripted workers of non-military and non-German backgrounds ordered, under threat of death or being sent to concentration camps, to do jobs close to the front. For his work with Ryzewski's engineering firm, he is given rations and a token payment of cigarettes and such. Wlad is interrogated by Ukrainian Camp Police. His teeth are knocked out by a rifle butt. When the doctor comes to dress his wounds he escapes. Wlad uses his underground alias, Wojciech Glodusz, and moves ahead of the Nazi push to the Ukraine. In Kiev Wlad meets a couple of former students from the Lwow Academy. They welcome him, remembering his friendship and resistance to the Nazis.

March 1942 When the Nazis arrive Wlad (as Wojciech Glodusz) is sent to help to paint decorations for all buildings in a landing strip in Vinnitsa with the firm of E Faidt, working as a varnisher. Around this time Professor Sichulski dies; Wlad recalled he was broken by the war.

May Wlad fetches Ludwik from Lwow to work as a housepainter. They fix houses and build camps throughout the district in the Ukraine.

24 August Wlad contacts Russians of Polish origin and becomes involved with the 6th Partisans Army Diversion Group of the Kiev area. Wlad, not using an alias, works for Adolf Rachow's painting and decorating firm. He secretly copies forms needed by the 6th Army Group on a hidden mimeograph. He receives and distributes the banned newspaper *Wytrwamy*.

September 1943 Wlad contracts bronchitis and is sent back to Lwow, and recovers at Ludwik's place at 11a Krzyzowa Street. The Ukrainian Police remember him and come looking for him. They soon close down the flat and shift them to a tiny unit on the 2nd floor of a house in Nicolas Kopernicus Street.

March 1944 Wlad meets a member of the Polish Underground Forces (AK), codenamed "Jan" and is sent to Krakow to meet Colonel Rulewicz. Subsequently he is employed at Tarnow, unloading construction wood from trains. He is ordered by the AK to take up a position as decorator with a German army store and to co-operate with another worker, codenamed "Krawiec" (Tailor). They send electrical motors, gasoline and oil on to Moscice. Wlad, codenamed "Marlarz" (Painter), works as a spy. His resistance work in Tarnow is top secret and he does not divulge any information to Ludwik. Wlad begins working for the Holy Cross Mountains Brigade of the NSZ, the second largest underground organization in Poland after the AK. His secretary Janina Starzyk works for the Nazi municipal government in Tarnow and is able to get papers, photographs and documents needed to smuggle refugees. He becomes well-known to the inhabitants of the Tarnow district, working mainly around the towns of Lysa Gora, Dabrowa, Klikowa and Tarnow itself. His unit resides in the forests and lives off the land.

April A bomb hits the rotunda and damages the steel and glass structure and some of the canvas panels of *Panorama Raclawicka*, a huge mural painted in 1893-94 by Jan Styka, Wojciech Kossak and several others, commemorating the popular uprising of 1794 led by General Tadeusz Kosciuszko. Depicting battalions of his horsemen life size, it is in two sections, each 57 metres long by 15 metres high, mounted on a specially constructed rostrum. A number of concerned artists, including Jan and Wlad, decide that the mural has to be taken down and hidden. Such a public statement of national pride would be considered provocative by the Nazi regime but the mural is in danger of being destroyed. Jan, and Wlad arrange the dismantling of the canvas panels. Jan works out where to cut the joins in the canvas, and they take a horse and cart to the square under cover of darkness. Assisted by other academics, who are aware of the mural's historical significance, and workers, they smuggle the panels to the basement of the Bernadine Church, where they had discovered a huge vault hidden by a wall which they had had to knock out. The mural survived the war and in 1984 was installed in a specially designed building in Wroclaw.

August Wlad and Ludwik are arrested by Nazi soldiers while the former is mimeographing papers with Janina in Lysa Gora. They are searched and taken to train carriages transporting Russian prisoners of war. Janina is taken elsewhere, her fate unknown. Wlad and Ludwik are transported initially to Auschwitz, then Pawlowice. Wlad's camp number is K.4.1000. He is lent to the firms of Hoch and Priz. They are put to work building a landing strip. He receives certificates for various handyman skills. Wlad remains active in the resistance field. He is interrogated regularly each month.

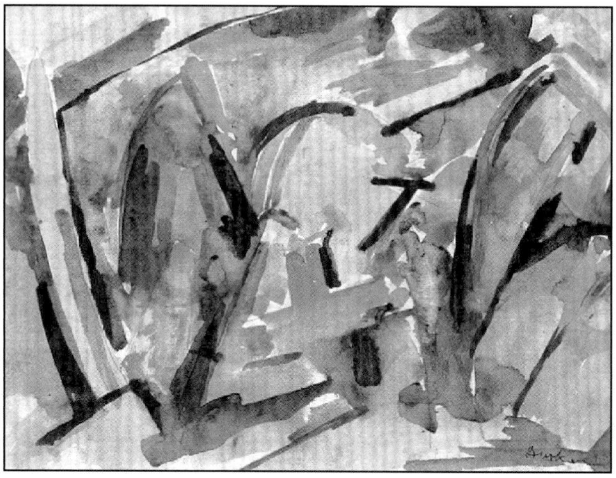

Murnau landscape. Watercolour on paper. 1945, Murnau, Germany. 24.5 x 33.0 cm. Dutkiewicz Archive.

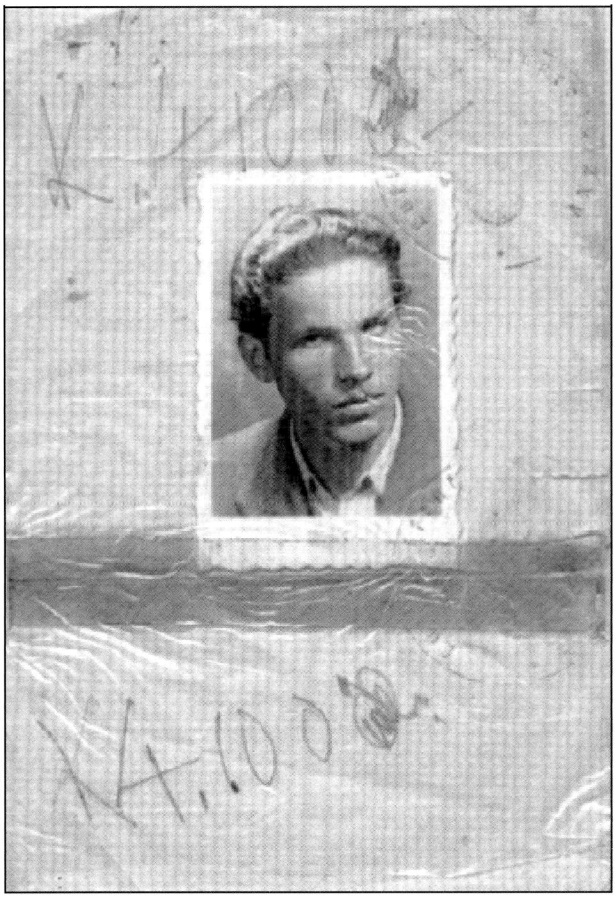

Concentration camp identity card, with list of interrogations and photograph. 1944-45. Dutkiewicz Archive.

January 1945 The Camp in Pawlowice is evacuated to Reisen Gebirgen, in the Glatz district, Czechoslovakia. Wlad is put to work building ramparts for tank barrages under a Polish Ukrainian Wladyslaw Jakubenko, who is able to organize work schedules and arrange military papers and passes for Wlad, Ludwik and himself. Wlad is lent out as a worker to the firm of Kuzyk from time to time. The interrogations continue.

May Wlad escapes with Ludwik, Jakubenko and another man in early May. They reach Prague during the insurrection against the Nazis. They are suffering from severe rashes under their arms and in their groins, and their feet are covered with enormous blisters. Czech partisans take them to Smolaga, a Polish restaurateur who is subsidising the uprising and has organized refugee escape routes. Smolaga keeps them at Konwitska, Prague-1 for six days. The doctor who examines them finds them suffering from inflammatory tumours in their feet caused by chilblains from their work in the labour camp and their flight, as the nights are still cold. They are hospitalised, while the Russian scouts move into Prague. Following a visit of a Russian officer to their ward they decide it is not safe to stay. They take clothing from a nearby corridor and walk out of the hospital. Wlad realizes they will not get far without papers, so he organizes the necessary details through Smolaga, a member of the *Narodny Komitet*, to cut through the red-tape. The document acquired indicates they are trying to get back to relatives in the Allied Zone. They board a train at Prague Central; for two days and one night the SS and military police check passengers, searching for German refugees, regarded by the Reich as traitors.

8 May Germany unconditionally surrenders. The territory through which the trio has to travel is the only land still occupied by Nazi troops. But they soon encounter Soviet patrols in the district and witness a Soviet slaughter of many refugees at the border. Smolaga's document gets them through.

20 May They arrive in Passau in Bavaria in Allied Occupied Zone and are taken by Allied soldiers to Hohenfels Displaced Persons Camp, outside Regensburg in Allied Germany.

June After screening, his oldest brother Stan, an exiled officer in the Polish army, arrives on a motorbike and pillions Wlad back to Murnau, an isolated and picturesque village south of Munich. He takes the aspiring painter to the home of Wassily Kandinsky's former partner, Gabrielle Münter, who is about fifty years old at the time. Known as the "Russian House" (*Russenhaus*), and later the *Münterhaus*, the "museum" had been Kandinsky's favourite working retreat and the couple's home before World War One. Wlad discusses Kandinsky's art and makes a small watercolour with Münter's paints (page 54). Wlad is appointed Camp Leader of No. 2 camp, responsible for 16,000 people. He sets about helping to establish new lives for the refugees. He sets up a theatre, a school and a church, which he designs. He establishes art classes for adults and children. He teaches most of the subjects in the school and works as a substitute priest until two priests eventually arrive from Dachau.

1946 He founds a troupe, *Teatr Nowy*, and writes most of the scripts, as well as painting sets and producing plays. But he runs into trouble with the camp authorities and regional International Refugee Organization officials over some of the content.

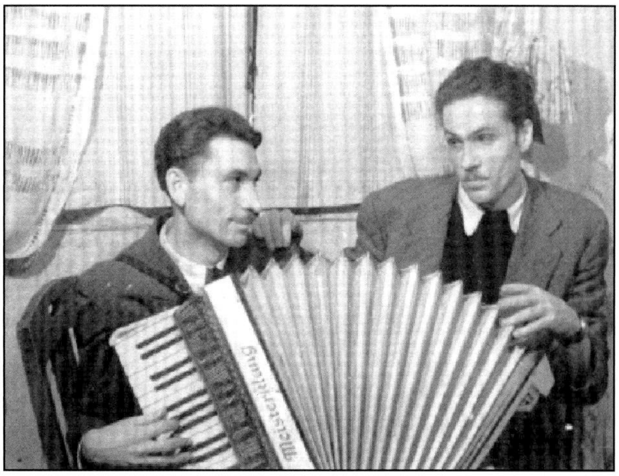

Wlad and Ludwik in Hohenfels Camp. Photograph. 1945, Hohenfels, Germany. Dutkiewicz Archive.

September 1946 Wlad exhibits at UNRRA's Displaced Persons Art Exhibition at Regensberg. He shows three oils: a self-portrait, and two complementary landscapes titled *Winter* and *Summer*. While visiting the Stadt Theater and Opera House in Nuremberg he attends some of the war crimes trials of Nazis, and meets the famous Polish-origin cartoonist and war artist, Feliks Topolski, who is then living in London and there to draw the trials. Topolski advises him that everything about character is discernible in the face, that everything is a potential subject for art, and that it may be comical. The contact between these two artists is as crucial as the contact Wlad made with Kandinsky's early abstractions: the influence on his drawing style is considerable.

1947 A contact in the Underground, Captain Slawek, leads his long-lost sister Cecylia out of Poland into the English Zone. They catch a train to the border with the American Zone, where they bribe an official to let them pass. The trip takes several weeks, and Cecylia arrives in Hohenfels to rejoin her brothers, bringing with her some documents and artefacts from the old family home. Disqualified of his DP status because of his anti-repatriation activities, Wlad is moved to the section of the camp complex put aside for prisoners, pariahs and malcontents. It is a frustrating year for Wlad as he tries to re-establish his reputation and connections with the AK and NSZ.

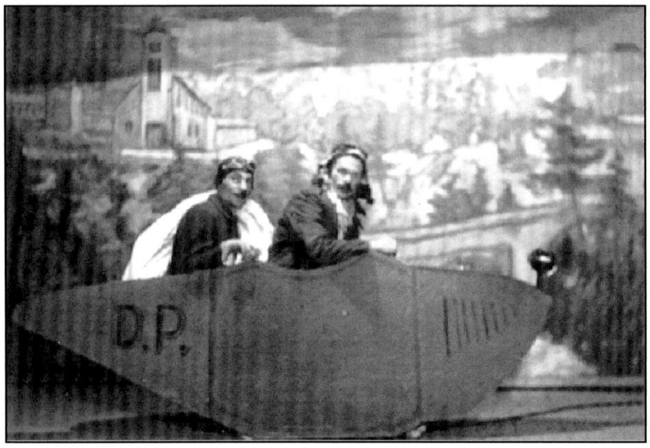

Ludwik and Wlad in Wlad's play *Repatriation to the Moon*. Photograph. 1946, Hohenfels, Germany. Dutkiewicz Archive.

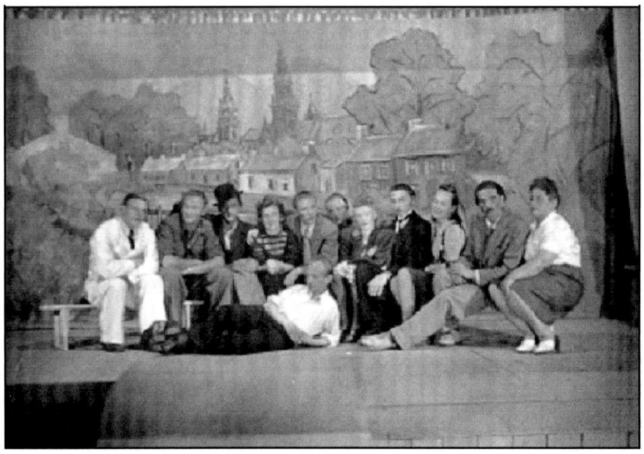

Wlad (second from right) and the players in *Teatr Nowy*. Photograph. c.1947, Hohenfels, Germany. Dutkiewicz Archive.

June 1948 *Teatr Nowy* has mounted one hundred and fifty productions in Hohenfels and on tours throughout Bavaria but through migration and repatriation of its performers and stagehands is in decline.

1949 Ludwik undertakes the necessary medical tests to migrate to Australia. He travels to Naples, where he boards the *General Omar Bundy*. Stan is summoned to again serve General Wieczorkiewicz, as his adjutant, and is stationed at Johnstone Castle camp in Renfrewshire, near Glasgow. A woman in IRO suggests a way out of Cecylia's dilemma over her dubious refugee status and increasing pressure to return to Poland. If she migrates to England, she can accept an offer to work for Courtaulds in London, which would grant her permission to stay in that country. It is the only means by which she can avoid repatriation to Poland. Cecylia settles in a hostel in Stourbridge, Worcestershire, and writes to Wlad. Stan writes to Wlad from London informing of his decision to return immediately to his family in Poland. Stan knows the implications of his decision but he loves his wife and she needs him with the family. The result is an awkward reception for Stan back in Poland and seven years of home detention. Cecylia tries to contact him but misses him by a matter of days. Wlad decides to follow Ludwik. When approved he sets off by train from the resettlement centre, heading through Austria to Italy. He stays in Naples for almost two months and finally boards the *Anna Salen* to head for Australia. Italian Customs explain that weight restrictions require him to leave most of the forty-three canvasses he had completed in Hohenfels and in Naples behind. He brings three or four unstretched canvases with him in the bottom of his suitcase.

24 August Wlad arrives in Fremantle and is taken with other DPs to a camp about five kilometres outside the town of Northam, about a hundred kilometres northeast of Perth.

1950 Plagued by a rare illness he moves to Adelaide for treatment and rejoins his brother. When recovered he is employed under contract to the state railways to paint the Adelaide Railway Station with Czech-origin artist Alex Sadlo. He meets his future wife Joan Watson and gets deeply involved in the local art scene. Quickly he becomes a Fellow of the RSASA and leading member of the CASSA and gets work as a set designer.

1951 His first major exhibition, with Ludwik, attracts rave reviews from Max Harris and Ivor Francis, and huge controversy through the conservative critics. He wins the inaugural CASSA Cornell Prize with *Summertime*. He also contributes the sets for *A Month in the Country* by Ivan Turgenev and *The House of Bernarda Alba* by Garcia Lorca.

1952 He holds an exhibition at Macquarie Galleries in Sydney with the assistance of the Arts Council of South Australia. He produces a series of forty watercolours for an exhibition in Adelaide and also shows in Melbourne.

1953 He marries Joan Watson and begins a successful partnership which provides a hub for artistic people in Adelaide, hosting regular soirees, parties and openings over the next two decades.

1955 He wins the CASSA Cornell Prize again with *Orient*. He is chosen as one of seven artists featured in the film *Painting 1950-1955 South Australia*. He paints several mural commissions and shows his first experiments in purely abstract painting (not expressionistic). He begins to develop a theory of art which is articulated by Brian Claridge.

1956 He wins The Advertiser Prize with *Travellers* (shared with Erica McGilchrist), and is commissioned to prepare murals and sculptures for the *Architectural Convention Exhibition* in June. But a motorcycle accident at that time leaves him with a fractured skull, loss of memory and no colour vision. He cannot paint. It stalls his painting career for four years and initiates a series of painful operations and outcomes. He has already held six major solo exhibitions and has one ready for the New Year. He has been a one-man revolution in South Australian art and by the end of the year is the father of two boys, with three girls to follow. With the devoted assistance of his wife and closest friends, especially Nancy Claridge, over the next few years he reconstructs his memory.

1958 He begins lecturing at the SA School of Art, having been sought out by the new Head, Paul Beadle. He partipates in *Survey 1*, National Gallery of Victoria and the inaugural *Helena Rubenstein Travelling Art Scholarship* exhibition, Art Gallery of New South Wales.

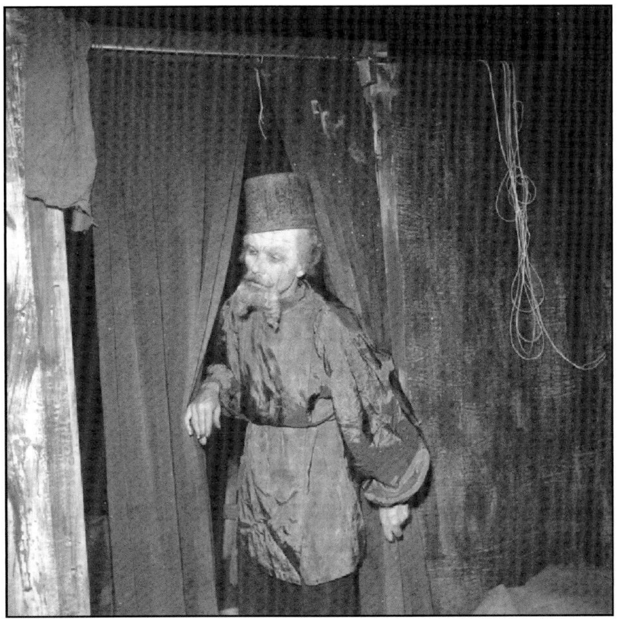

Wlad as Mikhail Ivanovich Kostylyov, landlord, *The Lower Depths*. Production photograph by Ian Davidson. Dutkiewicz Archive.

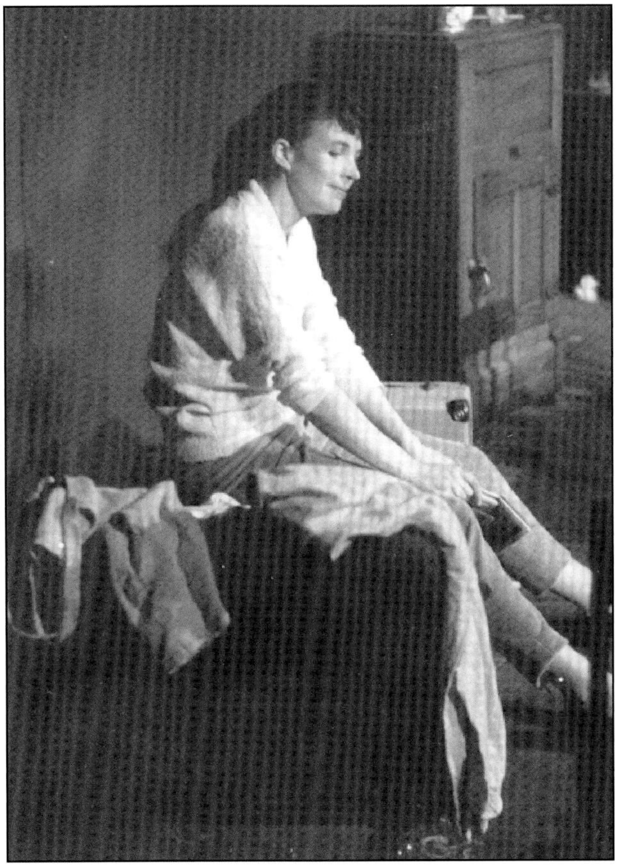

Barbara West as Beatie Bryant, *Roots*. Production photograph by Ian Davidson. Dutkiewicz Archive.

1959 Wlad re-engages with the theatre, and produces Jean Jacques Bernard's *The Unquiet Spirit* for Adelaide University Theatre Guild. He teaches Stanislavsky method at WEA and sets up a new troupe, the Art Studio Players. His contribution for the inaugural Adelaide Festival in 1960 is a production of Maxim Gorky's *The Lower Depths*, which Max Harris describes as a *tour de force*. ASP produces several more important plays, including national premieres, until 1962.

1960 Wlad resumes painting and enters his mature period, producing series after series of original and imaginative works in oil and watercolour in expressionist, abstract and semi-abstract modes. He then holds annual Christmas or Festival exhibitions in Adelaide and several exhibitions in Melbourne, Canberra and Sydney.

1961-62 He exhibits at Whitechapel Gallery in London and Raymond Burr Gallery in Los Angeles with survey exhibitions of contemporary Australian art. He produces as series developed from observing the touring Bolshoi ballet.

1964-66 For the Adelaide Festival he designs the stage décor for Hanka Rucinska, a Polish actress and choreographer who graduated from Krakow and had a connection with the regional Mazowsze Polish Folk Dancers. In the following year he produces three large panels on the Monte Cassino victory in WWII for the celebrations of the Polish millenium; then holds a major exhibition at Princes Hill Gallery in Melbourne.

1967-70 He produces Ibsen's *The Wild Duck* for Adelaide University Theatre Guild and then appears in several Crawford Production television dramas in roles written specifically for him by a former member of ASP, Terence Stapleton. His figurative art concentrates on family life, youth and the Mazowsze dancers.

1974-76 He holds a major survey exhibition at Lidums Gallery, Adelaide. Poor health and a badly injured hand curtail his painting career again, this time for nine years.

1985-89 Wlad resumes painting. Over the next few years he produces small series of oils pertaining to the Chernobyl disaster, the sesquicentenary of South Australia and Australia's bi-centenary. In 1988 he suffers an alcohol-related breakdown and undergoes rehabilitation. He then lives on his own in the city and continues to paint, working more with mixed media on paper. A major survey is held at Greenhill Galleries in the next year.

1990s He holds three more major survey exhibitions. His eyesight deteriorates and he has cataracts removed from both eyes in successive operations.

1999 He dies in Adelaide on 2 October, suffering from lung cancer.

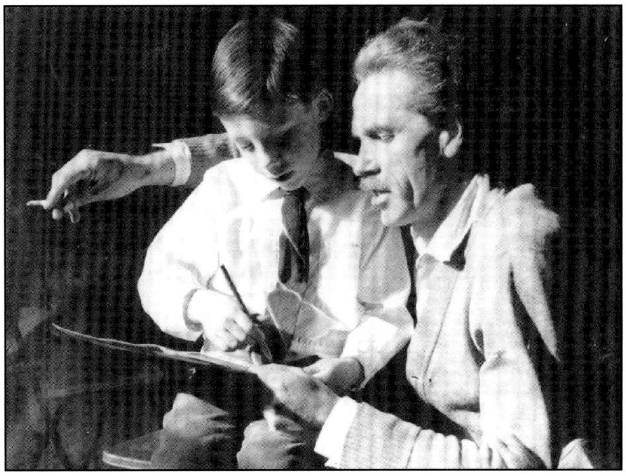

Wlad with his first-born, Michal. Photograph. ca.1961, Adelaide. Photograph courtesy News Ltd. Dutkiewicz Archive.

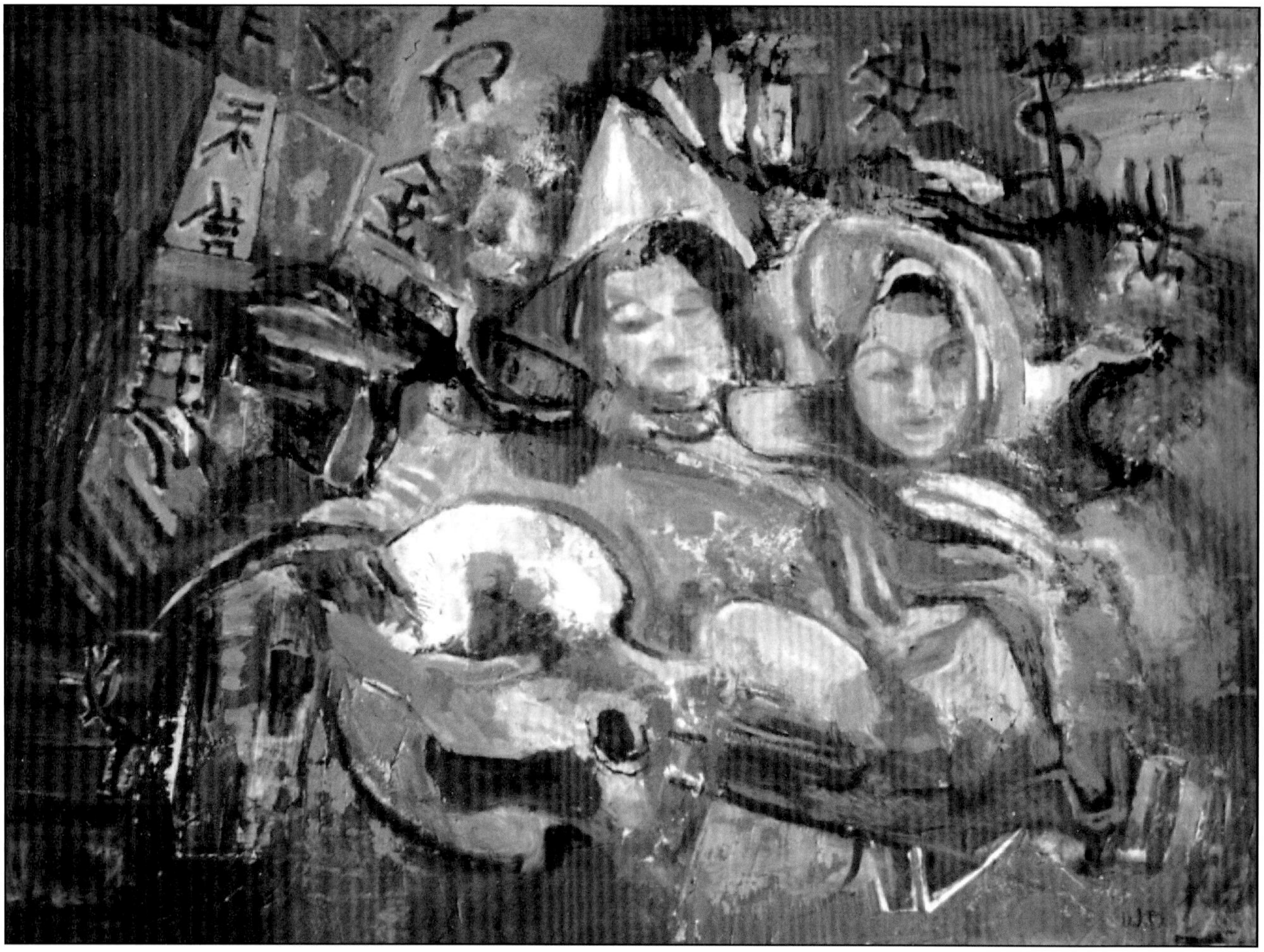

Asian friends. Oil on composition board. 1975, Adelaide. approx. 91.0 x 122.0 cm. Estate of the artist.

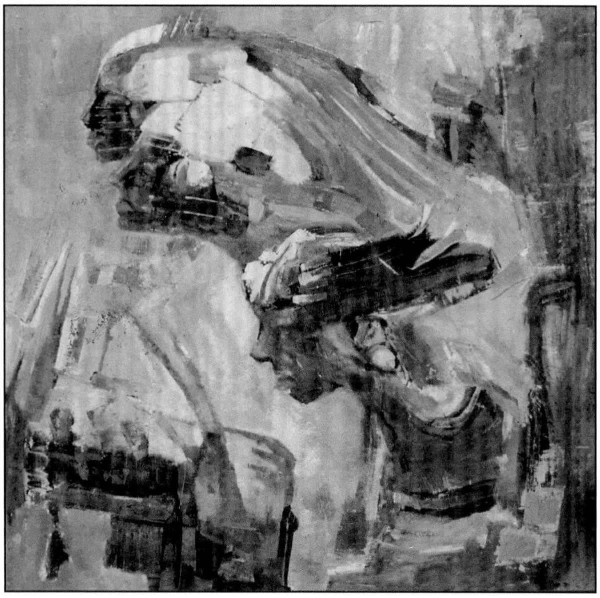

Papuans. Oil on composition board. 1972, Adelaide. approx. 90.0 x 90.0 cm. Collection unknown.

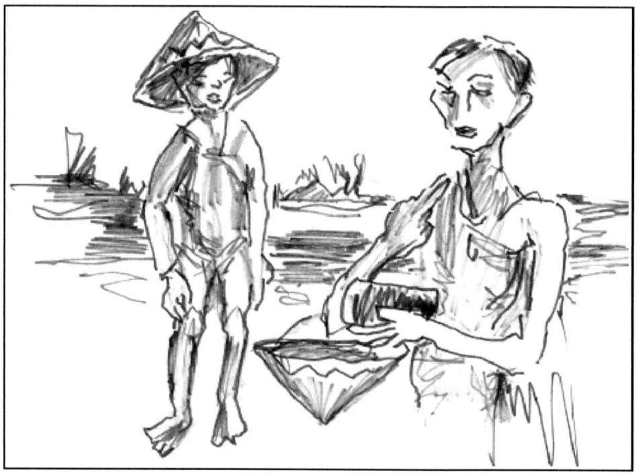

Preliminary drawing for *Pol Pot* series. Felt pen on paper. ca.1980, Adelaide. 20.6 x 26.0 cm. Estate of the artist.

Exhibitions & Awards

One-Man and Major Exhibitions

1.	Feb. 1951	with Ludwik Dutkiewicz, RSASA Gallery, Adelaide.
2.	June 1951	Curzon Gallery, Adelaide.
3.	June 1952	RSASA Gallery, Adelaide.
4.	July 1952	Macquarie Galleries, Sydney.
5.	June 1953	Peter Bray Gallery, Melbourne.
6.	Sept. 1953	New Gallery, Adelaide.
7.	May 1955	RSASA Gallery, Adelaide.
8.	Aug. 1957	RSASA Gallery, Adelaide.
9.	Mar. 1960	Twin Street Gallery, Adelaide.
10.	Aug. 1960	Australian Association for Cultural Freedom, Winnipeg, Canada.
11.	June 1961	RSASA Gallery, Adelaide.
12.	Mar. 1962	Studio Gallery, Adelaide.
13.	Nov. 1962	Jazz Gallery, Melbourne.
14.	Apr. 1963	Hutt St. Café, Adelaide
15.	Mar. 1964	Studio Gallery, Adelaide
16.	Mar. 1966	Studio Gallery, Adelaide.
17.	May 1966	Princes Hill Gallery, Melbourne.
18.	July 1966	with Ludwik Dutkiewicz, University of Adelaide Staff Club.
19.	Aug. 1966	Rostrevor College, Adelaide.
20.	Sept. 1966	El Dorado Gallery, Sydney.
21.	Oct. 1966	Jibilla Gallery, Adelaide; with Jo Caddy and Irene Hussin (pottery).
22.	Nov. 1967	Jibilla Gallery, Adelaide; with Irene Hussin (pottery).
23.	Mar. 1968	Studio Gallery, Adelaide.
24.	Mar. 1968	Street sculptures, King William Street, Adelaide Festival of Arts.
25.	Nov. 1968	Nundah Gallery, Canberra.
26.	Nov. 1968	Studio Gallery, Adelaide.
27.	Mar. 1970	Studio Gallery, Adelaide.
28.	May 1970	Russell Davis Gallery, Melbourne.
29.	Nov. 1970	Studio Gallery, Adelaide.
30.	Mar. 1972	Studio Gallery, Adelaide.
31.	Nov. 1972	Studio Gallery, Adelaide.
32.	Mar. 1974	Studio Gallery, Adelaide.
33.	June 1974	25th Anniversary Retrospective, Lidums Gallery, Adelaide.
34.	Mar. 1976	Studio Gallery, Adelaide.
35.	Dec. 1976	Studio Gallery, Adelaide; with sons Michal and Adam.
36.	Apr. 1977	State Library of South Australia with the State Theatre Company's production of Chekhov's The Cherry Orchard; with both sons.
37.	Dec. 1977	Polish Art Foundation, Melbourne.
38.	Aug. 1989	Forty Years in Review, Greenhill Galleries, Adelaide.
39.	Aug. 1991	Big Art, Hilton International Hotel/Reade Art, Adelaide.
40.	Mar. 1993	Political Works, RSASA Gallery, Adelaide.
41.	Mar. 1996	Paintings and Works on Paper 1950-1995, BMG Art, Adelaide.
42.	Apr. 2005	Wladyslaw Dutkiewicz (1918-1999): A Selection of Works from The Last Decade (1989-1999), RSASA, Adelaide.

Group and Mixed Exhibitions

1.	Sept. 1946	YMCA-YWCA UNRA Displaced Persons' Exhibition, Regensburg, Germany.
2.	July 1951	CAS Jubilee Art Show (winner of inaugural Cornell Prize for *Summertime*).
3.	Oct. 1951	CAS of Australia 13th Annual Interstate Exhibition, Education Galleries, Sydney (*Ensemble*, *Universalism*).
4.	Mar. 1952	Royal Adelaide Exhibition, Centennial Hall (winner of two silver medals, including for best painting, *Landscape*).
5.	Apr. 1952	Adelaide 1952 Group, RSASA Gallery (with Michael Brous, David Dallwitz, Ludwik Dutkiewicz, Ivor Francis, Jacqueline Hick, Stanislaus Rapotec, Douglas Roberts, Barbara Robertson, Francis Roy Thompson).
6.	July 1953	CAS Annual Exhibition (runner up to Cornell Prize with *Composition I*).
7.	Mar. 1954	Adelaide 1954 Group, Peter Bray Gallery, Melbourne.
8.	Aug. 1954	SA Painters in London, Artists International Association Gallery, London.
9.	July 1955	CAS Annual Exhibition (winner of Cornell Prize for *Orient*).
10.	1955	6th Dunlop Prize, John Martin's Gallery and touring (finalist, *Evening*).
11.	Oct. 1955	CAS 17th Annual Interstate Exhibition, Education Galleries, Sydney (*City*, *Horses in the paddock*).
12.	May 1956	1st National Critics' Choice Exhibition, National Gallery of Victoria.
13.	1956	Blake Prize exhibition, touring (finalist *Healing of the Sick*).

14.	June 1956	6th Australian Architectural Convention Exhibition, Botanic Park, Adelaide.
15.	Sept. 1956	The Advertiser Prize Exhibition, RSASA; *Travellers* joint-winner.
16.	Nov. 1956	Olympic Exhibition, Gallery of Contemporary Art, Melbourne.
	Nov. 1956	CAS 18th Annual Interstate Exhibition, Education Galleries, Sydney (*Christmas time*).
17.	Jan. 1957	Adelaide 1957 Group, David Jones Gallery, Sydney.
18.	June 1957	Adelaide 1957 Group, Gallery of Contemporary Art, Melbourne.
19.	Feb. 1958	Survey 1, National Gallery of Victoria; with John Coburn, Leonard Crawford, Frank Hodgkinson, George Johnson, Vincas Jomantas, Clifford Last and William Rose.
20.	Aug. 1958	1st Helena Rubinstein Travelling Art Scholarship, Art Gallery of New South Wales.
21.	Sept. 1958	Recent Australian Paintings, Farmer's Blaxland Gallery, Sydney.
22.	Mar. 1959	3rd Tasmanian Art Gallery Exhibition, Hobart (*City at night*).
23.	Mar. 1959	Art in Everyday Life, Legacy's Kelvinator refrigerators' auction, David Jones, Sydney.
24.	Mar. 1960	Contemporary Australian Art, CAS of SA, Charles Birks Gallery, Adelaide (*Hossanah* [aka *Hiroshima*]).
25.	Jan. 1961	Pequeno Gallery, Adelaide; with Ludwik Dutkiewicz, Lawrence Daws, David Dridan, Stan Ostoja-Kotkowski, Alex Leckie, Mervyn Smith, Jacqueline Hick, Anton Holzner, Ruth Tuck and Francis Roy Thompson.
26.	June 1961	Recent Australian Painting, Whitechapel Gallery, London (*Neon lights*).
27.	1961	Museum of Modern Art, Melbourne, artists included Hick and Holzner.
28.	July 1961	CAS Annual Exhibition (finalist in Cornell Prize with *Silence*).
29.	Nov. 1961	Australian Artists, Raymond Burr Galleries, Beverly Hills (*In orbit*).
30.	June 1962	New Influences, Newcastle City Art Gallery (*Corroboree*).
31.	Feb. 1964	CAS of Australia Annual Interstate Exhibition, Argus Gallery, Melbourne (*Landscape*).
32.	1964	Cornell Prize and Opening Exhibition, CAS of SA Gallery, Adelaide.
33.	Mar. 1966	An Exhibition of Paintings & Sculpture by Migrant Artists, Miller Anderson Gallery, Adelaide.
34.	Mar. 1966	South Australian Art Today, RSASA (*Grapepickers, Landscape in Ocean*).
35.	1966	Maude Vizard Wholohan Prize, RSASA, Adelaide (*Juggler*).
36.	Nov. 1967	Critics' Choice Exhibition, CAS of SA, Adelaide (*Fishermen*).
37.	Apr. 1970	Industrial Fair Exhibition, Melbourne.
38.	July 1971	CAS Survey '71 Exhibition, RSASA Gallery, Adelaide.
39.	Feb. 1973	Nicolas Copernicus Anniversary Exhibition, Dallas Brookes Hall, Melbourne.
40.	Apr. 1973	Nicolas Copernicus Anniversary Exhibition, National Bank Centre, Adelaide.
41.	Mar. 1974	International Art Exhibition, Pallottine Fathers, Kew, Melbourne.
42.	1974	South Australian Painters, Adelaide Festival Centre.
43.	Sept. 1975	Fine Arts Exhibition by Polish Artists, Adelaide.
44.	1978	The Masters Choice, RSASA, Adelaide (*Colour television*).
45.	Sept. 1978	50 Years of South Australian Art: 1928-1978, Art Gallery of South Australia.
46.	1981	Visions after Light: Painting in South Australia 1836-1981, AGSA.
47.	Oct. 1985	Modern Australian Painting, Charles Nodrum Gallery, Melbourne.
48.	Apr. 1986	Five Polish Artists in Adelaide, Adelaide Festival Centre.
49.	Nov. 1986	Jubilee 150 Polish Arts Exhibition, Dom Polski Centre, Adelaide.
50.	Apr. 1989	Abstractions, with Ludwik Dutkiewicz, Michal Dutkiewicz, Dave Dallwitz and Ron Orchard, Union Gallery, University of Adelaide.
51.	Aug. 1990	Mixed Exhibition, Charles Nodrum Gallery, Melbourne,
52.	Feb. 1991	Dutkiewicz Dutkiewicz Dutkiewicz, with Ludwik and Adam, Kensington Gallery, Adelaide.
53.	Feb. 1992	A Brush with the Stage, South Australian visual artists and the stage, 1930-1991, RSASA.
54.	Nov. 1992	Being Contemporary, Contemporary Art Centre of South Australia, Parkside (*Yellow fragment*).
55.	Dec. 1993	Four by Four Dutkiewicz: an exhibition of abstract paintings by Wladyslaw, Ludwik, Michal and Adam, Artists in Profile series, Adelaide Town Hall.
56.	Sept. 1994	Male Artists of South Australia 1895-1995, Kensington Gallery, Adelaide.
57.	Dec. 1994	Polish-Australian Artists 1945-1995, Pol-Art, Adelaide Festival Theatre.
58.	Dec. 1996-97	1956: Melbourne, Modernity and the XVI Olympiad, MOMA at Heide, Melbourne.
59.	Aug. 2003	20th Century Style: Furniture, Art Gallery of South Australia (*Calligraphy*).
60.	Oct. 2004	Exhibition of Multicultural Artwork (1945-1980), Multicultural Communities Council of South Australia, Adelaide.

NB There were other exhibitions for which no catalogues can be located.

Awards

Cornell Prize 1951 (*Summertime*); Bronze medal, Royal Adelaide Exhibition 1952, Silver medal, Landscape – oils; runner up Cornell Prize 1953 (*Composition I*); finalist Dunlop Prize 1955 (*Evening*); Cornell Prize 1955 (*Orient*); finalist Blake Prize 1956 (*Healing of the Sick*); The Advertiser Prize 1956 (*Travellers*); Gold medal, Best painting (*Landscape*); Silver medal, Figurative Painting (*Madonna*), Certificate of Merit, Australian Industrial Subject (*Nuclear reactor*), Certificate of merit, black & white graphic (*Kerosene stove*), Royal Adelaide Exhibition, 1957; finalist Maude Vizard Wholohan Prize 1966 (*Juggler*).

Collections & Commissions

The Vatican, Rome; *Zwizek Zolnierzy Narodowych Sil Zbrojnych*, Kalkow, Poland; The National Collection, now Artbank, Sydney; National Gallery of Victoria; Art Gallery of South Australia; Tasmanian Museum and Art Gallery; Newcastle Region Art Gallery, New South Wales; Hamilton Art Gallery, Victoria; State Library of South Australia; Flinders University Art Museum, Adelaide; South Australian Tourist Bureau; Adelaide Festival Centre Trust; Glenside Hospital, Adelaide; University of Queensland; State Bank, Adelaide; Margaret Carnegie, Melbourne; Hookers, Melbourne; Architectural Convention 1956; Charles Nodrum Gallery, Melbourne; Royal South Australian Society of Arts; Dom Polski Centre, Adelaide; YMCA, Adelaide; John Martin's Ltd, Adelaide; Fisher Jeffries, Adelaide; Piper Alderman, Adelaide; private collections in Australia, United States of America, Canada, United Kingdom, France, Japan, Venezuela and New Zealand.

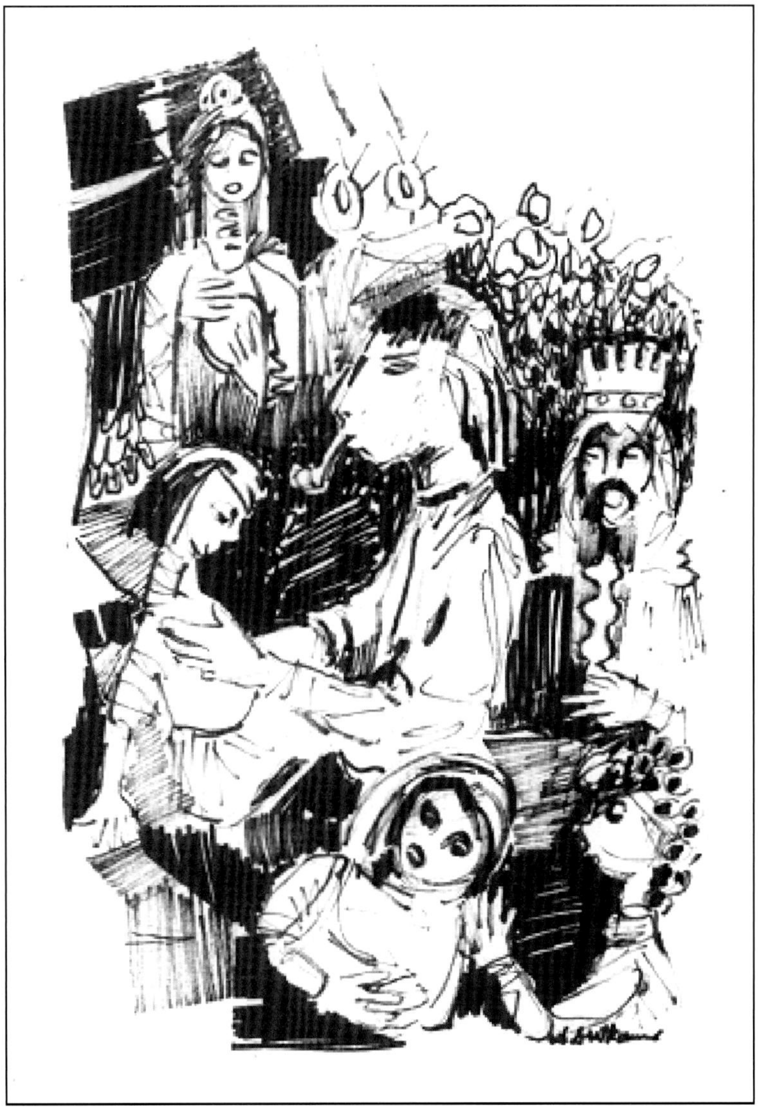

Puppet maker. Christmas pageant series. Felt pen on paper. 1973-74, Adelaide. approx. 50.0 x 39.0 cm. Private collection, Adelaide. Photograph: Graeme Hastwell.

Selected Bibliography

Books

Bonython, Kym (comp.). *Modern Australian Painting & Sculpture: A survey of Australian art from 1950 to 1960.* Foreword by Prof. Joseph Burke. Introduction by Laurie Thomas. Adelaide: The compiler, 1960. *Travellers*, b&w plate, 67.

Bruton, Dean. *Recollections – Contemporary Art Society of S.A. 1942-86.* Parkside: CAS, 1986.

Campbell, Jean. *Australian Watercolour Painters 1780-1980.* Adelaide: Rigby, 1983.

Davidson, Ian. *Art, theatre and Photography: Remembering Stan Ostoja-Kotkowski (1922-1994) in Adelaide, South Australia, 1954-1972.* Strathalbyn, SA: The author, 2000.

Gleeson, James. *Modern painters 1931-1970.* Australian Painting Studio series. General ed. John Henshaw. Dee Why West, NSW: Lansdowne, 1971.

Heathcote, Christopher. *A Quiet Revolution: The rise of Australian art 1946-68.* Melbourne: Text, 1995.

Hetherington, John. *Australian Painters.* Melbourne: F. W. Cheshire, 1963.

Hughes, Robert. *The Art of Australia.* 2nd ed. Harmondsworth, UK: Penguin, 1970.

Kandinsky, Wassily. *Concerning the Spiritual in Art.* George Wittenborn, New York, 1947.

________. *Point and line to plane.* New York: Solomon Guggenheim Foundation, 1947.

Luck, Ross K. A *guide to modern Australian painting.* Melbourne: Sun Books, 1969. *Travellers,* b&w plate.

Ouspensky, P.D. *Tertium Organum: A key to the enigmas of the world.* 3rd ed. Reprint. New York: Alfred A. Knoff/London: Routledge and Kegan Paul, 1951.

Reed, John (ed.). *New painting 1952-62.* The Arts in Australia series. London: Longmans, Green & Co., 1963. *Congregation,* b&w plate, 48.

Richardson, Donald. *Art & design in Australia: a handbook.* Melbourne: Longman Australia, 1995: 136-43.

Smith, Bernard. *Australian Painting 1788-1970.* 2nd ed. Melbourne: Oxford University Press, 1971.

Ward, Peter. *A Singular Act: Twenty-five years of the State Theatre Company of South Australia.* Kent Town, SA: Wakefield Press, 1992.

Dictionary and Encyclopaedia entries

Benko, Nancy. *Art and Artists of South Australia.* Foreword by Ivor Francis. Adelaide: the Lidums family, 1969. *Actors,* b&w plate, 50.

Kroeger, John. *Renniks Australian Artists.* Introduction by Dion H. Skinner, ed. Adelaide: Renniks & Co., 1968.

McCulloch, Alan (comp.). *The Encyclopedia of Australian Art.* 1st ed. London: Hutchinson, 1968. *Shapes in Space,* colour plate, 336a.

McCulloch, Alan and Susan McCulloch (ed.). *The Encyclopedia of Australian Art.* 3rd ed., rev. and updated. St. Leonards, NSW: Allen & Unwin, 1994.

Parsons, Phillip & Chance, Victoria (eds.). *The Companion for the Theatre in Australia.* (Sydney: Currency Press, 1995).

Journal articles

Baily, John. "The Maude Vizard-Wholohan Prize exhibition." *Kalori* 4, no. 3 (Sept. 1966). Discusses *Juggler,* 11.

Bulletin of the National Gallery of South Australia 17, no.4, serial no. 64 (April 1956). *Waterholes,* b&w plate, 5. Biographical Details by Mary Barwell.

_________. "Wladyslaw Dutkiewicz – Art Studio." *Ivor's Art Review* 4, no. 5 (March-April 1960), 10.

Cato, Nancy. "Art in South Australia." *Australian Letters* 2, no. 4 (March 1960): 67-78.

Claridge, Brian. "Wladyslaw Dutkiewicz – Society of Arts." *Ivor's Art Review* 1, no. 11 (September 1957): 24.

Claridge, Nancy. "Adelaide Group – David Jones, Sydney." *Ivor's Art Review* 1, no. 5 (March 1957): [10].

Cleland, Pamela. "Contemporary Art Society – Institute Building." *Ivor's Art Review* 1, no. 6 (April 1957):[2].

Davidson, Ian. "Survey of Recent Theatre décor by S. A. Artists," *Ivor's Art Review* 3, no. 1 (November 1958): 2. *The House of Bernarda Alba,* b&w plate.

Dutkiewicz, Wladyslaw. "Ian Fairweather." *Kalori* 3, no. 4 (December 1965): 14.

Francis, Ivor. (ed.), *Ivor's Art Review,* November 1956-March/April 1960.

_____________. "Comment," *IAR* 2, no.7, (May 1958): 14.

_____________. "Cornell Prize," *CAS Broadsheet* (summer 1961): [2].

[____________]. "(Sur)prizes!" *IAR* 1, no.1 (November 1956): [1]. Article regarding the Advertiser Prize.

[____________]. "Wladyslaw Dutkiewicz." *IAR* 1, no.2 (December 1956). *Waterholes,* b&w plate.

Galbally, Ann. "Melbourne and the 1956 Olympiad." *Art and Australia* 34, no. 4 (winter 1997): 462-63.

Heathcote, Christopher. "Days of Hope." Review of "The Europeans." Canberra: NGA, 15 March-9 June 1997. *Art Monthly Australia,* no. 99 (May 1997): 29-30.

Ivor's Art Review 2, no.7 (May 1958). Photograph with caption regarding sale of picture to National Gallery, Hobart.

Ivor's Art Review 2, no.8 (June 1958). Review, CAS at RSASA Exhibition.

Ivor's Art Review 2, no.12 (October 1958). Article regarding commissions for Ostoja-Kotkowski and W.Dutkiewicz to decorate fridges as a result of Helena Rubinstein Exhibition and W.Dutkiewicz's mural commission.

Jew, Betty (ed.). "Meet the artist: Wladyslaw Dutkiewicz." *Kalori* 7, no. 1 (March 1969): 8-10. *Cascade* and *Sisters,* b&w plates.

Luck, Ross. "A Momentous Occasion." *CAS of S.A. Broadsheet* (November 1954): 1-2.

McCulloch, Alan. "Migrant Artists in Australia." *Meanjin* 14, no. 4 (no. 63, 1955.): 511-16. See also errata in *Meanjin* 15, no.1: 97.
Missingham, Hal. "Recent Australian Painting." *Studio* 153, no. 767 (February 1957): 33-41, 63.
Neylon, John. "Wladyslaw Dutkiewicz." *Artlink* 19, no. 4 (Summer 2000).
Nicholls, Christine. "Wladyslaw Dutkiewicz 1918-1999." *Art and Australia* 38, no. 2 (December 2000): 233.
Northcote, H. [Hugo] Stafford. "Art and Architecture." Reproduced from the Advertiser. In *CAS of S.A. Broadsheet* (July 1956): 3-5.
"Sixth Australian Architectural Convention Exhibition, Botanic Park, Adelaide." *Architecture and Arts* (August 1956): 24-31. Black and white photograph showing W. Dutkiewicz sculptures *in situ* and painting (also cover).
Sokolowska, Basia. "Histories in Transition." Five Polish artists – Maximilian Feuerring, Stanislaw Ostoja-Kotkowski, George Olszanski, Wladyslaw Dutkiewicz, Ludwik Dutkiewicz. ed. Dynah Dysart. *Art and Australia* 30, no. 4 (winter 1993): 488-93. *Bush* (1951), b&w plate.
Tarrant, Deborah. "Critics cornered." *Australian Art Collector* 1 (July-September 1997), 61-65. *Ice creams*, colour plate.
Trumble, Angus. "Adelaide: A School for Scandal." *Art and Australia* 37, no. 3 (March 2000): 389-97.
Ward, Peter. "Theatre in Adelaide from 1920 to 1960." *Australian Letters* 2, no. 4 (March 1960):98-102.
Young, Elizabeth. "Criticisms of South Australian Art Today." *Kalori* 4, no. 2 (June 1966). b&w photograph of exhibition, 15.
Zongollowicz, Bogumila. "Nie spelnione ostatnie marzenie." *Polish Kurier*, no. 139 (October-November 1999): 31-32.

Unpublished articles and theses

Claridge, Brian. ["The art of Polish-Australian painter Wladyslaw Dutkiewicz."] Unpublished article for *Kultura*, Paris. TD, L ca.1955. Dutkiewicz archives/AGNSW Library/AGSA Library.
Dutkiewicz, Adam. "Raising ghosts: Post-World war Two European Émigré and Migrant Artists and the Evolution of Abstract painting in Australia, with special reference to Adelaide ca.1950-65." (Adelaide: University of SA, 2000).
Dutkiewicz, Adam & Stephanie Schrapel. Unpublished text and text for display panels for the exhibition *Wladyslaw Dutkiewicz: Political Works*. Adelaide: RSASA, 1993. AGSA Research Library/AGNSW Library/Art and Artists Australia files, State Library of Victoria.
Francis, Ivor. Goodbye to the City of Dreams – an autobiography. Unpublished manuscript, ca.1990. Ivor Francis Bequest. AGSA Research Library. [Published by AGSA, 2004].
Loveday, Thomas. "The Painter's Space." In "Abstract Pictorial Space." Master's thesis. University of Sydney, 2001.

Films, Television Performances and Videos

"Love is a Silver Chain," *Homicide*, December 1967.
Ostoja-Kotkowski [sic], J. Stanislaw. *Painting 1950-55 South Australia.* 1955. 25 minutes [16mm. Colour film featuring] … Mervyn Smith, Jacqueline Hick, Francis Roy Thompson, Ludwik Dutkiewicz, Stanislaus Rapotec, Douglas Roberts, Wladyslaw Dutkiewicz. Directed and produced by J. Stanislaw Ostoja-Kotkowski. Commentary written by H. Stafford-Northcote and spoken by Roy Leaney. [Film] Photography by J. Campbell Dobie, [stills photography by Ostoja-Kotkowski]. Music by Bill Holland. Transcript copy [of text] by Paula Furby, printed 8 November 1990. Mortlock Library of South Australiana.
Ostoja-Kotkowski [sic], J. Stanislaw. *Architectural exhibition.* 1956. 20 minutes, colour film group no.919/1/3. Mortlock Library of South Australiana.
"Poor Anna," *Homicide*, April 1969.
"The Krystina File," *Hunter*, November 1968.
"Zemsta," *Homicide*, November 1966.
David, Roger. *Five minutes with Wlad.* ca.1997. 6 minutes. DVC/16mm, b&w/colour documentary film. Flinders University Production. Winner: Best Documentary, 1998 National Student Film Festival, Sydney; Best Documentary, 1999 National Amateur Video Awards, Cairns; Selected for Screening and Finalist, Amnesty International's 1998 Bombard Film Festival, Brisbane; 1999 Woodford Film Festival; 1999 Atom Awards, Melbourne. Reviewed Independent Filmmakers (December-January 1998).

About the Authors

ADAM DUTKIEWICZ was born in Adelaide on Christmas Day in 1956. In 1997 he was awarded a scholarship by the University of South Australia to undertake a doctoral degree at the South Australian School of Art in visual art history and theory. His thesis was titled *Raising ghosts: Post-WWII European émigré and migrant artists and the evolution of abstract painting in Australia ca.1950-1965.*

He began his tertiary education with a Bachelor of Communication Studies in the 1980s and completed his Honours year in 1991. From 1979 until 1985 he edited and published the arts magazine *Words And Visions* (*WAV*) for 18 editions and published several books under the imprint, including the collected stories of Flexmore Hudson, a children's fiction anthology, *The Land of Ideas*, and several poetry titles.

In 1989 he prepared the 40th anniversary exhibition for his father at Greenhill Galleries, Adelaide, and another at Hilton International Hotel in Adelaide in 1991. He produced three further retrospective exhibitions of his father's art, in 1993, 1996 and 2005, the former and latter at the Royal South Australian Society of Arts and the other at BMG Art.

From June 1992 until November 2005 he worked as art critic for *The Advertiser* newspaper and has also worked as a freelance critic and writer for *Business Review Weekly* and *Art Monthly Australia* online. He has also been the author of numerous major catalogue essays and a contributing author for the monograph *Franz Kempf: Thinking on paper* (2002) and author of *Mervyn Smith: Watercolours* (2004).

He has exhibited his own paintings in prominent commercial galleries and public spaces, with his first major exhibition at the RSASA in 1992. He was shortly thereafter elected President, an office he held for two terms. He then coordinated *Polish-Australian artists 1945-1995* for the Adelaide Festival Centre. Since then he has held exhibitions at BMG Art, Adelaide Central Gallery and Adelaide Institute of TAFE, and twice in Sydney. He is represented in the Mortlock Library of South Australiana and the Glenside Hospital collection and in private collections locally, interstate and overseas.

JOHN JEFFERSON BRAY AC was admitted to the South Australian Bar in 1933, becoming a Queen's Counsel in 1957. In 1967 he was appointed directly to the post of Chief Justice by Premier Don Dunstan, a position he held until 1978, when he retired from the Supreme Court bench because of heart trouble. He was an outstanding lawyer and thinker whose reputation spread throughout the legal world. Dr. Bray was Chancellor of the University of Adelaide from 1968 to 1983, and a keen classical scholar and humanist. He wrote a number of works of poetry and was patron of the Friendly Street poets. He was the longest serving member of the Libraries Board of South Australia, serving from 1944 to 1987, and was honoured by having the Bray Reference Library of the State Library of South Australia named after him in 1987. He was known for his classical scholarship, poetry and wit, as well as his large and diverse circle of acquaintances. He died in 1995. For a detailed view of his life see Wilfred Prest (ed.), *A Portrait of John Bray: Law, Letters, Life* (Kent Town: Wakefield Press, 1996).

BRIAN CLARIDGE was a practising architect who was Secretary, Vice-President and Acting-President of the Contemporary Art Society of South Australia in the early 1950s, and before his death in 1979 was a Senior Lecturer in Architecture at the University of Adelaide. He was an advocate of inventive, environmental architecture and one of a generation of innovators in the field, which included John Morphett, Keith Neighbour, John Chappel, Robert Dickson and Newell Platten. His writing on architecture was published often, and today can be seen as prophetic, both in terms of its endorsement of Jørn Utzon and other like-minded pioneers and its insistent dismissal of brutalism and economically rationalist styles.

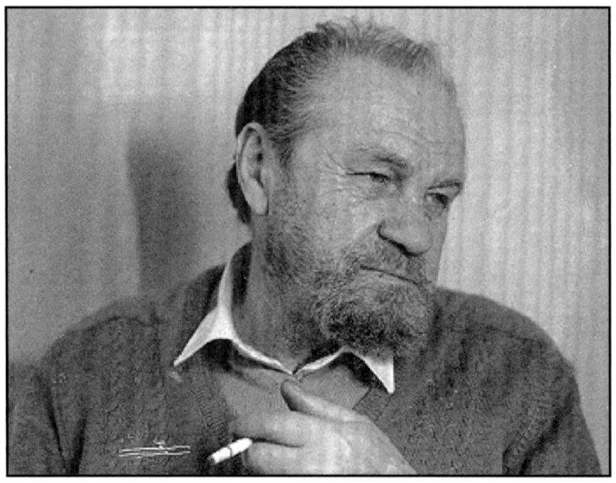

Wlad at home. Polaroid photograph. 1989, Adelaide.
Courtesy Greenhill Galleries, Adelaide.